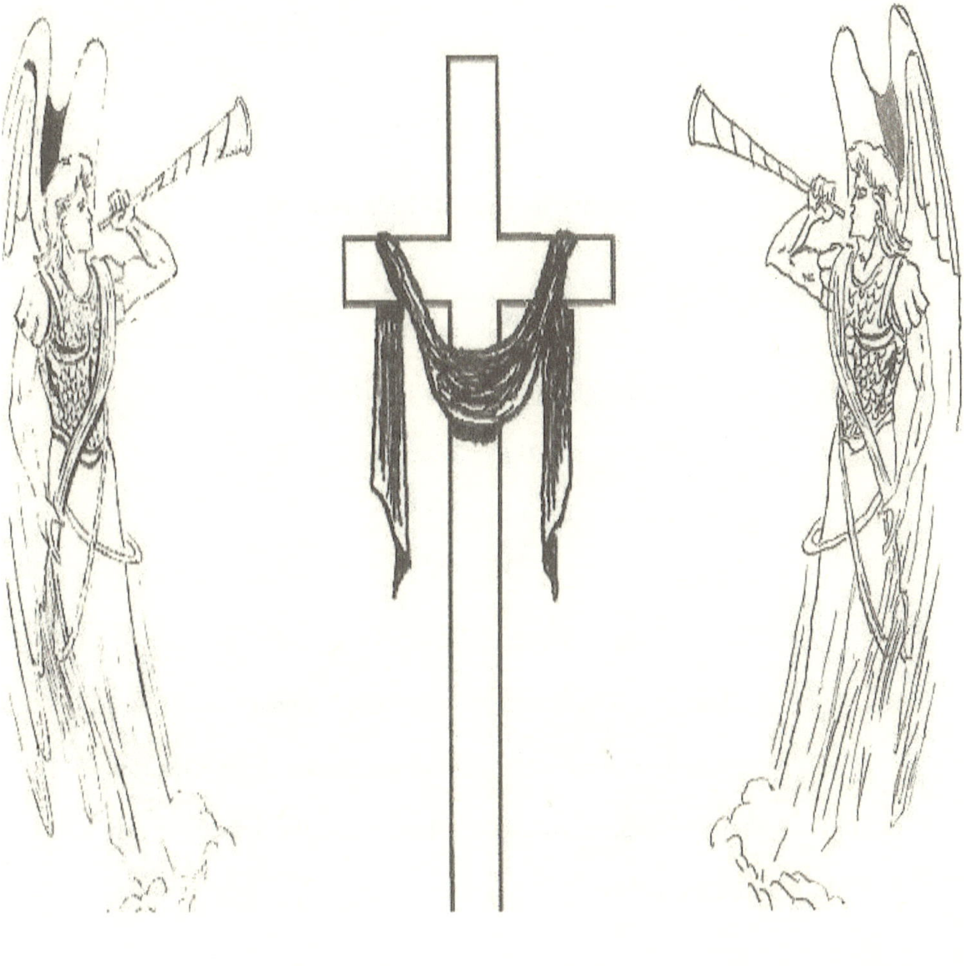

The Eternal Purpose

Written by David B Hathcock

CONTENTS

Part One

The Primal Creation: Heaven and Earth; "the world that then was" Gen. 1:1 and 2

Peter 3:6

Satan's Rebellion: The earth became waste and in ruin; Gen 1:2God created it not in

ruin. Isa 45:18

Part Two

The earth restored and blessed: "the heaven and earth which are now." Gen. 1:2-31;

2 Peter 3:7

Satan Enters and the Consequence: Gen. 3:1-24

Mankind Dealt with as a Whole: Gen. 4:1-11:26

The Chosen Nation Called and Blessed: Gen. 11:27 - Mal. 4:6; JHVH Rejected, Israel Scattered.

Part Three

The First Advent: Micah 5:2, Zech. 9:9. The Four Gospels; Romans 15:8; the King and the Kingdom Proclaimed and Rejected, and the King Crucified.

The Kingdom Re-proclaimed. Acts 3:19-20. The Church of God Called and Taken Out: Acts 13 and Following verses, and Earlier Pauline Epistles. The Kingdom again rejected and Israel again scattered.

The Kingdom Postponed and in Abeyance: "Not yet" Hebrews 2:8. The Later, or Prison Epistles (Pauline). The Mystery Revealed and Proclaimed. Eph. 3:2-11, Coil. 1:25; 2:2-3. 1 Tim. 3:16. The New Hope. Phil. 3:11-14, Titus 2:13.

Part Four

The Second Advent. The First Resurrection; The Kingdom Established. The King Enthroned; The day of the Lord. Matt. 24 & 25:31, Luke 19:11-27, Isa. 2:11-19, Joel 2 and Following.

The Chosen Nation Recalled and Blessed: Romans 11:11-36, Acts 15:16, Isa. 60, 61, 62, Jer.30 & 31, Zech. 12, 13, 14.

Mankind Dealt with as a Whole: Joel 3:2, Matt. 25:31-46, Acts 15 thru 17, Rom. 15:8-12, Rev. 4 thru 19.

Part Five

Satan Bound and the Consequences: Rev. 20:1-3

The Earth Restored and Blessed. Rev. 20:4-6, Isa. 35; The Millennium.

Satan's Final Rebellion: Rev. 20:7-10, Followed by the Second Resurrection and the Judgment of the "Great White Throne". The Destruction of all Things That Offend. Rev. 20:11-15.

Part Six

The New Heaven and the New Earth: The Day of the Lord. Rev. 21, 22; 2 Peter 3:12-13; Isa. 65:17, 66:22.

The Eternal Purpose

Introduction

This work is given in love. It's intended to show the love of God the Father to his children. My hope is that by reading these pages God's children will have a better understanding of the purpose for their lives in God creation. This work is mainly done for the "Elect" of God; the ones God has called for special purposes and sent through this earth age to perform certain functions in order for this world to continue as God wants it too. It's an effort to help open the eyes of God's elect to the great work still before them and help in preparing their minds against the deception in the world and the greater deception coming in the near future.

Please don't misunderstand me about "God's Elect". These people are not special in the sense of having "things" better in this life. These are just ones who have been judged and justified by God before he brought them into this world. I'll have more to say about what the Elect are and where they were justified later on in this writing.

I'll talk about a time period on this earth before mankind as a whole populated it. I call this time period the 'first earth age' for lack of a better description. In this respect, I'll refer to this present time period we are living in as the 'second earth age' in order to keep the two separated. Which leaves me to call the period of time after this world has ended, the 'third earth age', instead of as we usually refer to it as the 'eternity'. There will be more about this later on in my deliberations.

In my queries of the different earth ages, I'll refer to the flesh age or physical age at different places. These ages are the same as the second earth age. Only the words differ occasionally to better relate the meaning and because of needed emphasis on the subject matter being discussed. I have used these expressions in order for my readers to better separate the present world (age) from a time period when God's children weren't living in a flesh or physical body.

Some of my readers will not grasp the true significant of what they are reading at the first of this book and may want to lay it aside, but I strongly urge you to keep reading and maybe God will open your mind to his truths. God declared in his letter to his children that he has closed some of his children's eyes and ears so they cannot know what the scriptures mean. As it is written,

> And he said, go, and tell this people, hear ye indeed, but understand not; and see ye indeed, but perceive not. Make the heart of this people fat, and make their ears heavy, and shut their eyes; lest they see with their eyes, and hear with their ears, and understand with their heart, and convert, and be healed. (Isaiah 6:9-10)

Christ expanded on these writings of Isaiah in the book of Matthew,

> Therefore, speak I to them in parables: because they seeing see not; and hearing they hear not, neither do they understand. (Matt. 13:14)

And also, as it is written,

> And Jesus said, for judgment I am come into this world, that they which see not might see; and that they which see might be made blind. And some of the Pharisees which were with him heard these words, and said unto him, are we blind also? And Jesus said unto them, if ye were blind, ye should have no sin: but now ye say, we see; therefore, your sin remains. (John 9:39-41)

In simple terms, a child who does things which displeases his father and receives punishment for his acts will not be disciplined as sharply as the child who has been warned repeatedly and still does things contrary to his father's wishes. The child who doesn't know and does thing innocently will hardly receive punishment at all. God is fair and is not looking to punish his children; therefore, he has blinded some of his children so they don't fully understand what is taking place in this earth age. This way they are not judged as yet and will have the Millennium to be taught and learn the true purpose of their lives. For those of you who are not familiar with the 'Millennium' term; it is the period set aside by God at the end of this present world age. This period will last a thousand years; hence the term 'Millennium'.

God would be unfair if he condemned some of the peoples on this planet for not following and living by his laws when they have no idea what the laws are. Some have already died in the flesh and returned to the Father and never knew there was a creator or anything outside of where they lived. Would it be fair to send all these peoples to Hell? Whatever the situation; God is always fair in his judgments.

So, strange as it may seem, God doesn't want all of his children to understand what's happening in this flesh age of the world. You see, as long as you don't grasp the full plan of God, you're not held accountable for all your actions. Regardless of what preachers and teachers of God's word tell you, most of God's children will be saved in the Millennium, which takes place after this flesh age ceases to exist. There will be enough people whom God has called and opened their mind to the truth of Jesus Christ for his purpose to be accomplished in this age and the rest will taught in the Millennium.

The words written herein are for you to learn the natural events which are to take place in the normal order of God's plan and to find where you fit in this plan. By knowing circular history, you are able to recognize the events which have happened as the bible foretold. And by seeing these things as they have happened in history, should give you confidence to trust your Father's written word on the coming events, which will take place in the life of most of my readers yet to come.

Some of you have always known there was more to God's word then what you were being taught in church.

Christ servant,

David B Hathcock

Part One

The Primal Creation: Heaven and Earth:

In the book of Revelation, we are told, "God created all things for his pleasure." (Rev. 4:11) The New Testament book of Ephesian teaches us that God created all things by Jesus Christ. (Eph. 3:9) the gospel of John states, In the beginning was the word and the word was with God, and the word was God. The same was in the beginning with God. All things were made by him; and without him was not anything made that was made. (John 1:1-3) So, you should have grasped the obvious truth; God = Holy Spirit = Jesus Christ, known by the Christian world as the "TRINITY". There is only one God, three different functions or personalities; but only one God. Is this statement hard to comprehend? Let's look at it another way. We are all three different people or roles which we assume daily. First, we are children of our mother and father and play the role of a child in their presents. Also, when we marry, we have a role to play as a husband or wife to our spouse. And then, when children of our own arrive, we become guardians and care takers. Each role carries its own action and results, but we remain one person. My relationship with my parents is not the same as with my wife or with my children. Nor, is my relationship with my wife the same as with my children. And of course, my relationship with the children is totally different from the way I act with either my wife or my parents.

From the Bible in John 4:24, we are informed by Christ, "God is a Spirit and they that worship him must worship him in spirit and truth." Since God is a spirit, he is also invisible to the human eye. (Now into the King eternal, immortal, "invisible", the only wise God, be honor and glory forever and ever. Amen 1Timothy 1:17) and again, (Who is the image of the invisible God, the Firstborn of every creature: Col. 1:15) And being invisible to his creation, gave credence to certain men the idea of non-existence. Chief among these men and also leader was Satan, or Lucifer, or the Devil, or a Dragon, or Serpent, and a host of other names. Satan is the one credited with leading the rebellion against God in the first earth age or the span of time before God brought men in fleshly bodies to live on earth. In this rebellion, Satan convinced a third of God's children to follow him with the goal of overthrowing God's Kingdom and authority. Rev. 12:4-9.

We are told very little of this rebellion. It is mentioned in only a few places in the bible. And if you are not a careful reader, it might miss your attention all together. The easiest place to know there was a first earth age is given in 2 Peter: "For this they willingly are ignorant of, that by the word of God the heavens were of old, and the earth standing out of the water and in the water: whereby the world that then was, being overflowed with water, perished: but the heavens and the earth which are now, by the same word are kept in store, reserved unto fire against the day of judgment and perdition of un godly men. 2 Peter 3:5-7" Some so called scholars teach this was Noah's flood, but Noah's flood didn't destroy the earth or bring about all things being perished. There were people and a whole bunch of animals on board the ark. When the dove was sent out from the ark, a green twig was in the dove's mouth when it returned. So you see the world was not destroyed; only a lot of evil was done away.

Another place is in the book of Jeremiah.

We learn from the Bible that heaven and the earth were created by God. We just don't know the exact date. Genesis 1:1 read, "In the beginning God created the heaven and the earth". That's all it says in the book of Genesis. It doesn't say when or how long ago. When you hear preachers, Sunday school teachers, or any other person claim the earth was created 6000 years ago, you are listening to a lie. The lie is not intentional but comes from believing mathematical figures of people using biblical scriptures to try to set a correct date for the time of Adam and Eve's sojourn in the "Garden of Eden". The dates to Adam could be right, but the error comes in their thinking Adam was the first man created in this flesh world we live in today. (Flesh world means people with flesh or physical bodies' verses people with spiritual bodies.) NOT SO! The first man and woman created by God in this flesh world were of the ethnic races as stated in Genesis 1:27. It reads, "So God created man in his own image, in the image of God created he him; male and female created he them". The Hebrew word translated "man" is "Adam" and only means a human being or the species "mankind". This is not the same man God created in

Genesis 2:7 where it reads. "And the Lord God formed man of the dust of the ground, and breathed into his nostrils the breath of life; and man became a living soul". In this verse the Hebrew word for "man" is not the same as in verse 1:27 of the book of Genesis. This verse reads "Eth-Haadam" and means, "the man Adam" which is a different creation from the first man and woman created in Genesis 1:27. Most of the bible scholars of today know what I'm saying is true; they are just afraid to make it public for fear of losing some of their congregation.

So, you see, God created the races quite a bit before Adam came into the picture. Why? I don't know; I can't begin to think as God does. I'm sure he had his reasons. If we were to guess, there could be all kinds of paths we might take. To me, the most logical would be to find out first how this new mankind would fair in this physical world. Remember, God planned on bringing his children through this flesh world quickly and then giving them a spiritual body so they could return unto him. But we all know Satan messed that idea up.

The second verse of Genesis has been badly mistranslated. The error lies in the first part of the verse where it reads, "And the earth was without form and void". The word "was" is the mistranslation of the Hebrew word "hayah" which means "be", "become" "come to pass", "became". The correct translation reads, "And the earth became without form and void; and darkness was upon the face of the deep". So, you see something happen to cause the earth to become "without form and void". God tells us in Isaiah 45:18 he did not create the earth in vain or void. The verse reads,

> For thus saith the Lord that created the heavens; God himself that formed the earth and made it; he hath established it, he created it not in vain, and he formed it to be inhabited: I am the Lord; and there is none else. (Isaiah 45:18)

Who was this earth created "to be inhabited" by? From the book of Job, we learn the sons of God shouted for joy at the creation of the earth. Do you know who the sons of God are? Well, let's see; Jesus Christ is called the son of God and of course the angels are referred to as the sons of God, and then there is Adam of the Garden of Eden. Adam is called a son of God. That's it; these are the only sons of God and for these children the earth was created. Oh, I forgot Satan; he is also a son of God, but, I didn't really forget him or leave him out. He's just one of the angels who turned bad from too much pride. These sons of God, also called the children of God, were created before this second earth age or physical age began. But Jesus and Adam are the exception; Jesus in spiritual form has always been with God and Adam was created physically and one of the sons of God was then placed into his physical body. In essence, all were with God before this physical world (age) began. We'll discuss the physical and spiritual more as we go along and before you finish this material, I think you'll have a correct understanding of all the events leading up to your present life span.

When did all this take place? God asks Job almost the same question:

> Where wast thou when I laid the foundations of the earth? Declare, if thou hast understanding. Who hath laid the measures thereof, if thou knowest? Or who hath stretched the line upon it? Whereupon are the foundations thereof fastened? Or who laid the corner stone thereof; when the morning stars sang together, and all the sons of God shouted for joy? (Job 38:4-7)

Let it sink into your thinking, there was a vast time period on this earth before Adam and Eve ever came into existence. I refer to this period as the 1st earth age, since this period was millions or perhaps billions of our years long. The bible even tells of the dinosaurs and other prehistoric animal during this period. And, as the scriptures state to us,

> Behold now the behemoth, which I made with thee; he eats grass as an ox. Lo now, his strength is in his loins, and his force is in the navel of his belly. He moves his tail like a cedar: the sinews of his stones are wrapped together. His bones are as strong pieces of brass: his bones are like bars of iron. He is the chief of the ways of God: he that made him can make his sword to approach unto him. Surely the mountains bring him forth food where all the beasts of the field play. He lies under the shady trees, in the covers of the reed, and fens. The shady trees cover him with their shadow; the willows of the brook compass him about. Behold, he drinks up a river, and hast not: he trusts that he can draw up Jordan into his mouth. (Job 40:15-23)

In this discourse with Job, God can only be talking about the dinosaur; for no other animal can even come close to this description God gives at this time.

During this vast span of time God's children roamed the earth and enjoyed fellowship with their Father and the blessings he provided for them on this earth and the rest of the universe. They were created with bodies which never wore out; their bodies were very similar to the bodies we'll have in the Millennium when this flesh age or second earth age is over. This is the reason archaeologist can't find the "missing link". It doesn't exist! Haven't you ever wondered why the models built by archaeologist from the bone fragment they dig up look so much like an ape or monkey? They looked like a monkey because the fragment came from a monkey. A footprint has been found in stone which dates over two hundred thousand years ago. It looks like modern mankind footprints, but there was nothing around which even resembled modern humans two hundred thousand years ago. Who made the footprint? It's just more proof God's children which we know as angels today were made of solid material.

So, what happened? Where are the people that left the footprint so many thousands of years ago? We find in Ecclesiastes, the words of God which tell us,

> The thing that hath been, it is that which shall be; and that which is done is that which shall be done: and there is no new thing under the sun. (Eccl. 1:9)

In the book of Jeremiah, we have God speaking through Jeremiah. He tells the people why Jerusalem will be destroyed. But as we read, we begin to see God is really speaking about another event which happened during the first earth age. God is actually telling of the rebellion Satan led in the first earth age to replace God on his throne. (Jeremiah 4:18-27)

We know Satan led a rebellion against God and his government as stated in the book of Revelation. In chapter 12, we are told Satan led a third of God's children away in deception. And now, in Jeremiah, we see a little more of God's thoughts and what he did because of the rebellion. Also, we learn in the book of Psalms, he changed his children into spirits (Psalm 104:4) and removed them off of the earth and into a separate area from physical earth. I refer to this place as "Heaven" or another "dimension". Now don't go science fiction on me, because this place is real as the ground under your feet. You just can't see into this realm as yet. God has placed a veil or curtain over our eyes so we can't see or know a lot about this place. Evidence is given in Genesis with the "Garden of Eden" story and the Cherub's flaming sword to guard the entrance into this realm. Another example is given in 2 Kings, chapter 6: it reads,

> And when the servant of the man of God was raised early, and gone forth, behold, a host compassed the city both with horses and chariots. And his servant said unto him, alas, my master! How shall we do? And he answered, fear not: for they that are with us are more than they that are with them. And Elisha prayed, and said, Lord, I pray thee, open his eyes, that he may see. And the Lord opened the eyes of the young man; and he saw: and, behold, the mountain was full of horses and chariots of fire round about Elisha. (2 Kings 6:15-17)

Proof of this fact is shown in the scriptures in Genesis and we read,

> And it came to pass, when men began to multiply on the face of the earth, and daughters were born unto them, that the sons of God (angels) saw the daughters of men that they were fair; and they took them wives of all which they chose. And the Lord said my spirit shall not always strive with man, for that he is flesh: yet his days shall be hundred and twenty years. There were giants in the earth in those days; and also after that, when the sons of God came in unto the daughters of men, and they bare children to them, the same became mighty men which were of old, men of renown. (Genesis 6:1-4)

Everybody knows it's impossible to procreate without a solid substance no matter how you do it unless you are the living God. Angels are not gods but are created beings-the same as flesh men only their bodies were not flesh. I don't know what they were made of, but these 'angel bodies' were so similar to flesh that the very food angels ate to sustain themselves also sustains flesh bodies. The manna which fed the children of Israel in the wilderness after being released from Egypt was called "manna", and the bible states it was the food of angels. The bible tells us,

> Though he had commanded the clouds from above, and opened the doors of heaven, and had rained down manna upon them to eat, and had given them of the corn of heaven. Man did eat angels' food: he sent them meat to the full.   (Psalm 78:23-25)

The Israelites lived off manna (angels' food) for forty years while they wandered in the wilderness.

Additional evidence of angels having solid bodies is given in Genesis. Specifically, in verse eight we read,

> And he took butter and milk and the calf which he had dressed, and set it before them; and he stood by them under the tree, and they did eat. (Genesis 18:1-8)

These verses describe our Lord and two angels coming to visit Abraham before they continued their journey to destroy Sodom and Gomorrah. Archaeologist state modern man has only been around a little over fifteen thousand years or since the last ice age and they are right. Strange as it might seem to you; this data corresponds with what the bible states. Perhaps, you are wondering how this could be? You have forgotten the difference between God's time and man's time. God states one day to him is as a thousand years and a thousand years are as one day in 2 Peter 3:8 and Ps. 90:4. When you add the six days (6000 years) of God rejuvenation of the earth as given in Genesis 1:3-31 plus the day he rested (1000 years) and the eight day (1000 years) when "the Adam" was created up until present time (7000 years), you'll come up with about fifteen thousand years which will put this second earth age beginning a little after the last ice age and about when evidence of modern man is truly found on the earth.

So, what happened to ruin this paradise God created for his children? Pride! And Sin! And an angel called Satan who wanted to be God.

Satan's First Rebellion:

The second verse of Genesis lets us know the earth became void and without form. (Genesis 1:2) So now we need to find out why the earth became "void and without form". We are not told when Satan rebelled against God in the bible, just that he rebelled. Maybe the rebellion took place a little at a time until God could stand it no more. We know from his word that God is long suffering and patient with his children. And since, Satan is one of God's children; I'm sure it took a long time before God condemned him and pronounced a death sentence on him. In fact, God had made him ruler of earth before his fall into sin. Satan had been elevated to the position of one of God's anointing cherubs. So, what happened to him? Pride! He wasn't satisfied with the blessings God gave him. He wanted more! He wanted to take God's place and sit on the throne of God. But let's read the way the bible tells it. In the twenty-eight chapter of Ezekiel, we read of Satan's downfall. In the bible, Satan is referred to as the King of Tyrus which is a play on words, because tyrus translated from the Hebrew means "rock". He is not our rock. Our "Rock" is Christ as it is written in the first book of Corinthians:

And they all drank the same spiritual drink: for they drank of that spiritual Rock that followed them; and that Rock was Christ. (1 Cor. 10:4)

Starting with verse 12 in chapter 28 of the book of Ezekiel, we read,

Son of man, take up a lamentation upon the King of Tyrus, and say unto him: Thus saith the Lord God; thou sealest up the sum, full of wisdom, and perfect in beauty. Thou hast been in Eden the garden of God: every precious stone was thy covering, the sardius, topaz, and the diamond, the beryl, the onyx, and the jasper, the sapphire, the emerald, and the carbuncle, and gold: the workmanship of thy tabrets and of thy pipes was prepared in thee in the day that thou was created. (Ezekiel 28:12-13)

God gave us these verses in Ezekiel to let us know he doesn't do anything halfway. When he created Satan, nothing was spared to make him the best of everything to be had in His new creation. He was given the best mind, the best looks, the best voice, the best position in this world as ruler-second only to the creator. Reference is made to the "Garden of Eden" in the above description of the King of Tyrus so there can be no misunderstand. Satan is the one being described in these verses and not an actual flesh and blood king of Tyrus. Let us continue on with the description of Satan's downfall. Continuing we read,

Thou are the anointed cherub that covereth; and I have set thee so; thou wast upon the holy mountain of God; thou hast walked up and down in the midst of the stones of fire. Thou wast perfect in thy ways from the day that thou wast created, till iniquity was found in thee. By the multitude of thy merchandise they have filled the midst of thee with violence, and thou hast sinned: therefore, I will cast thee as profane out of the mountain of God: and I will destroy thee, O covering cherub, from the midst of the stones of fire. (Ezekiel 28:14)

We're going to break this down a bit and put what we've just read in today's speech so it'll be easier to understand. When God's word speaks of the cherub that covereth, we are to understand the phrase means Satan was to guard the mercy seat or the throne of God from any and all attacks. It's sort of like being the best man at a wedding. Of course, Satan wanted to sit on the throne instead of just guarding it. He thought he was better qualified to rule than the one to whom it belonged. Who did it belong to? Naturally the answer is Jesus Christ or, if you can grasp it, God himself in solid form. God gave Satan everything he needed to rule this earth and his children, but his pride was his downfall. He forgot to rule in mercy, love, and compassion. He chose to exalt himself and to follow the "get" way of life. The "get" way of life is what we are all born with in this physical age. It means we all want something from somebody. It could be your parents, your mate, or even where you work. This person never thinks about what they could "give" to the ones in need or how to "give" to make life better for another person. Most of the world is divided into either a "get" way of life or a "give" way of life. Christ is head of the "give" way of life and Satan is head of the "get" way of life.

Satan even wanted to be worshipped as God. He became selfish and conceited. His thinking was such to where he believed he could defeat God and replace the one who was entitled to sit on the throne with none other than himself. The throne or mercy seat was created for Christ to sit on and rule, but even he had to earn the right to it. This he did by allowing himself to be crucified for the sins of the Father's children-that is, the ones who repented of the sins they committed. God allowed Satan freewill just like he did for all his children. God allows all his children to have freewill in order to show them there is no way they can qualify to be in God's kingdom on their own, without help from God. The apostle Paul illustrates this in the Corinthians where we read,

> Now all these things happened unto them for ensamples; and they are written for our admonition, upon whom the ends of the world are come. (1 Cor. 10:11)

All the heroes and all the villains and the things they did are shown in the bible for us to learn to do things according to the way God wants it done. We can have a happy life and be blessed of God if we trust him. By placing our faith in Him to see us through hard times, we can be assured we'll never be let down. Even if the results are not what we expected and not the way we perceived the problem needed to be solved, God is still in control. When we try his way, he'll kick the rocks out of our path and make the way smoother and easier.

Now let's continue in the book of Ezekiel and Satan's downfall. We read,

> Thine heart was lifted up because of thy beauty; thou hast corrupted thy wisdom by reason of thy brightness: I will cast thee to the ground; I will lay thee before kings, that they may behold thee. Thou defiled thy sanctuaries by the multitude of thine iniquities, by the iniquity of thy traffick; therefore, will I bring forth a fire from the midst of thee, it shall devour thee, and I will bring thee to ashes upon the earth in the sight of all them that behold thee. All they that know thee among the people shall be astonished at thee: thou shall be a terror, and never shalt thou be any more. (Ezekiel 28:17-19)

Satan knew he was very handsome. Because of his looks and station in God's kingdom, he thought he was better than everyone else. Remember the expression, beauty is only skin deep. That which is in a person's heart is where the true beauty or ugliness lies. Satan is very smart; probably the smartest person who has walked this earth besides God in the form of Christ. Satan had a problem; he knew he was smart-smart to the point he didn't take time to hear all the arguments brought to him for judgment from his subjects. He rendered his decisions without thought of the truth. After all, he was in charge and he knew best or so he believed. What did God think of the way Satan handled business? He kicked his butt out of office and will lay him in the dust before kings the bible tells us in the above scripture. Because Satan is so wicked and such a deceiver, God has stated he will destroy him. God will destroy him from within and turn him into ashes in the sight of mankind. This destruction will take place after the Millennium and Satan will be no more. In the last part of Revelation, we read,

> And when the thousand years are expired, Satan shall be loosed out of his prison, and shall go out to deceive the nations which are in the four quarters of the earth, Gog and Ma'gog, to gather them together to battle: the number of whom is as the sand of the sea. (Rev. 20:7-10)

Satan was not alone in his rebellion. He was not a one-man destructive entity. He had lots of help. In Revelation 12:4 the number of God's children who followed Satan in this rebellion against the Father is revealed. In this book of Revelation, symbols are used to convey God's thoughts. There, Satan is symbolized as being a great red dragon with seven heads and ten horns. The heads and horns are symbols of the different offices he

holds and are not to be taken literally. The verse reads,

> And his tail drew the third part of the stars of heaven, and did cast them to the
> earth: and the dragon stood before the woman which was ready to be delivered,
> for to devour her child as soon as it was born. (Rev. 12:4)

Keep in mind this verse is all imaginary and symbolizes the nature of Satan. We'll

learn later on in this discussion just how beautiful Satan's outward appearance is, but for

now we are concerned with a third of God's children following Satan in a rebellious war

against God and God's followers. What did God do about this rebellion?

The book of Isaiah says,

> Behold, the Lord makes the earth empty, and makes it waste, and turns it upside
> down, and scatters abroad the inhabitants thereof. (Isaiah 24:1)

It was Satan's rebellion that caused God to make the earth to become "void and

without form". As it is stated in other places also, the Lord destroyed everything on the

earth; he changed his children into spirits and removed them from the earth as such. This

second verse (Isaiah 24:2) shows God doesn't play favorites. This chapter twenty-four

reaches from the first earth age all the way into the second earth age. Part of this chapter

twenty-four speaks of things even in the Millennium. This second verse reads,

> And it shall be, as with the people, so with the priest; as with the servant, so with
> his master; as with the maid, so with her mistress; as with the buyer, so with the
> seller; as with the lender, so with the borrower; as with the taker of usury, so with
> the giver of usury to him.

God doesn't leave anybody out, does he? Where do you fit in? Maybe, you're just like me as one of the people who doesn't have much going for them; but God included us in this same wipe out in the first earth age. Do you know why? If you are not working against something, then you are for it. So, nobody is innocent and God reads minds. What does God say?

> He that is not with me is against me; and he that gathers not with me scatters abroad. (Matthew 12:30)

For our study, we'll continue on in Isaiah chapter twenty-four with the next three verses:

> The land shall be utterly emptied, and utterly spoiled: for the Lord hath spoken this word. The earth mourns and fades away, the world (age) languishes and fades away; the haughty people of the earth do languish. The earth also is defiled under the inhabitants thereof; because they have transgressed the laws, changed the ordinance, broken the everlasting covenant. Therefore, hath the curse devoured the earth, and they that dwell therein are desolate: therefore, the inhabitants of the earth are burned, and few men left. (Isaiah 24:3-6)

I'm sure some of you are very good biblical scholars and will say these verses are describing what will happen at the end of this earth age. And you are right, but, don't forget what the scriptures tell us in the book of Ecclesiastes,

> The thing that hath been, it is that which shall be; and that which is done is that which shall be done: and there is no new thing under the sun. (Eccl. 1:9)

Also think about the end of the flesh age for a few minutes, the earth will not be empty at the end of this age. All people will be changed into a different form-a spiritual body to last the Millennium. This scripture describes the end of the events leading up to God's destruction of the first earth age.

This reference to being "burned" in the above verse is symbolic of the Holy Spirit changing his children into sprit form. (Psalms 104:4) A few were left as they were because they sided with God against Satan's rebellion. Some refused this change and fled God's presence. This is what Jude was conveying in his book about the "angels who kept not their first estate". We'll take a look at this verse in Jude,

> And the angels which kept not their first estate, but left their own habitation, he
> hath reserved in everlasting chains under darkness unto the judgment of the great
> day. (Jude 1:6)

The word "habitation" is the misleading word. It is translated from the Greek word "oiketerion" and actually means a spiritual body. The word "left" from the above sentence which is translated from the Greek word "apoleipo" translates to "left behind". The true meanings of Jude's words are that some of the angels refused God's offer of amnesty and to have their solid bodies changed into spirit form. After this change, these angels would then be born through flesh woman into this physical world. The ones who refused "left their spiritual bodies behind" and fled God's presence. Later, they joined up with Satan and entered this flesh world and impregnated the daughters of Adam to help Satan thwart the plan of God. Their first estate was the earth and they couldn't keep it because God destroyed it and everything in it. When this happened, these angels fled to some other place. Where? I don't know, but they are coming back. This is what Paul mentions in 1 Cor. 10, where he states, "For this cause ought the woman to have power on her head because of the angels". We know Satan and his bunch will be kicked out of Heaven as described in Revelation 12:7-9, but also the other "angels" who fled God's presence will be coming back. I don't know whether they will be subservient to Satan or not. They may fight against him and his allies for all I know. But whatever the case, the bible tells us that Christ will return quickly and put everything under his control and authority. (Rev. 18:11-21)

These verses in Revelation seem to support others in Isaiah. So we'll look at what they have to say about the first earth age. We read,

> The new wine mourns, the vine languishes, and all the merry hearted do sigh. The mirth of tabrets ceases, the noise of them that rejoice ends, the joy of the harp ceases. They shall not drink wine with a song; strong drink shall be bitter to them that drink it. The city of confusion is broken down: every house is shut up, that no man may come in. There is a cry for wine in the streets; all joy is darkened; the mirth of the land is gone. In the city is left desolation, and the gate is smitten with destruction. When thus it shall be in the midst of the land among the people, there shall be as the shaking of an olive tree, and as the gleaning grapes when the vintage is done. They shall lift up their voice; they shall sing for the majesty of the Lord; they shall cry aloud from the sea. (Isaiah 24:7-14)

New wine is expected to have flavor and strength and be exciting to the taste; this wine doesn't-meaning it's symbolic of the people. The people are sad, no "mirth" or "joy". They are wasting away and there is no trust in anyone or thing anymore. Everybody is waiting to see how God will judge them and the penalties they will receive because of their part in the attempted rebellion. Their old ways of life are gone. There's nothing left for them to salvage. They can only plead to the Lord for mercy. The offenders are so many it looks like a sea of people. But God won't listen. It's too late! He has turned a deaf ear to his children. Now God will put into action His plan for the second earth age.

> Wherefore glorify ye the Lord in the fires (East) even the name of the Lord God of Israel (Israel translated = God will rule) in the isles of the sea. From the uttermost part of the earth have we heard songs, even glory to the righteous? But I said, my leanness, my leanness, woe unto me? The treacherous dealers have dealt treacherously; yea, the treacherous dealers have dealt very treacherously." (Isaiah 24:15-16 emphasis mine)

Yes, God speaks in the above verses to go ahead and sing praises to Him and do it all over the earth. But God says it won't do you any good. You've waited too late. The treacherous dealers (priest and leaders) have led you astray. They were supposed to have given correct advice and answers from God; but they didn't and now it's too late. Just like it was in the days of Noah when the rains started and God shut the door to the ark, the people cried out to him but it was too late. And so it was in the first earth age; remember,

> The thing that hath been, it is that which shall be; and that which is done is that which shall be done: and there is no new thing under the sun. (Eccl 1:9)

This verse is probably where we get our saying, "what goes around comes around". God's word shows the correct lifestyle to live and be happy during your stay here in the flesh, but God also gives you freewill to do as you please. With a little imagination, you could picture your life as a ship you own. You have the right to sail it anyway that pleases your taste. You could sail it right into the "Lake of Fire" if you so choose, but why would you die when you can sail your ship along with God's people and live a beautiful life forever. The choice has always been yours.

In the next few verses, God speaks through the prophet Isaiah to explain what happens to the rebels who refuse to accept his way of life:

> Fear, and the pit, and the snare, are upon thee, O inhabitant of the earth. And it shall come to pass, that he who flees from the noise of the fear shall fall into the pit; and he that comes up out of the midst of the pit shall be taken in the snare: for the windows from on high are open, and the foundations of the earth do shake. The earth is utterly broken down, the earth is clean dissolved; the earth is moved exceedingly. The earth shall reel to and fro like a drunkard, and shall be removed like a cottage; and the transgression thereof shall be heavy upon it; and it shall fall, and not rise again. (Isaiah 24:17-20)

Who is the inhabitant of the earth? It's certainly not one of God's obedient children because they have all been removed from earth and changed into spirits. As it happened in the first earth age, similar action will take place at the end of this second earth age. We have such a person that is described as coming out of the pit in the book of Revelation. (Rev. 17:8-11) His name is Satan and he will be caught in his own snare because he thinks he's got everything under control. He's being feed enough rope until he hangs himself as the old saying goes. Why? Because when God pronounces judgment on a person, there is no appeal court to go to. Satan has already been tried and sentenced for all the transgressions he's committed through the centuries. He is the one being described as falling and not rising again. So, in these few verses, we have moved from the first earth age to the end of the second earth age.

Since we have moved to the end period of the second earth age, we read of judgment starting to be carried out.

> And it shall come to pass in that day, that the Lord shall punish the host of the high ones that are on high, and the kings of the earth upon the earth. And they shall be gathered together, as prisoners are gathered in the pit, and shall be shut up in the prison, and after many days shall they be visited. Then the moon shall be confounded, and the sun ashamed, when the Lord of hosts shall reign in Mount Zion, and in Jerusalem, and before his ancients gloriously. (Isaiah 24:21-23)

Now, we have jumped from the first earth age to the end of the second earth age. "In that day" is the Lords day or the Millennium and we see the Lord will punish the host of the high ones that are on high. We can get a better understanding of what God is describing in the book of Hebrews; so let's look there for a few minutes. In the twelfth chapter of Hebrews we read,

> Whose voice then shook the earth: (talking about the 1st earth age) but now he hath promised, saying, yet once more I shake not the earth only, but also heaven." (Hebrews 12:26, parenthesis mine)

This shaking of heaven takes place when Satan and his bunch are tossed out of Heaven by Michael and his angels. You can find this tossing out in Revelations 12:7-9. After Satan and his cohorts rule earth for a short spell by claiming to be the Christ, the real Christ will return and lock Satan up into the bottomless pit for the next thousand years.

The Kings of the Earth, mentioned earlier are known as Political, Education, Financial, and Religion. Don't ever forget them because they rule the Earth at present. When Christ returns, the kings will be eradicated and will no longer be with us any more Why, because there won't be any need for them again. Politics will be out the door because Christ is in charge and will rule fairly for all eternity. Religion will be the same for everybody and the love and worship of Christ will be the only way of life. There will no longer be financial burdens because money or any barter system will never be used again. Our Heavenly Father will provide for all our needs through Christ and all will have joy and peace of mind. Education is no longer required because all minds will be opened. The people will all know everything there is to know.

What else has happened because of Satan's rebellion? For one thing sin was brought into the world and now all the sons of God have a choice to make. They can choose to sin or not to sin. They can choose to follow either God or Satan. God's children have always had the option of sinning or not sinning, but the thought had just never occurred to them not to obey God's commandments. Until Satan chose to disobey and persuaded others to follow him, none disobeyed God. What I'm talking about is summed up in the old saying, "a rotten apple in a barrel of good apples will spoil a whole barrel of apples unless the rotten one is destroyed before it can contaminate the others". As in Satan's case, he hasn't been destroyed yet and he has made a lot of the sons of God rotten to the core. The angels who have not sinned in the first earth age didn't just up and become sinners, but the idea had been planted. Even after God had transformed their solid bodies into spirit form, some decided to leave God's presence and go their own way. But when they came to earth in this second earth age, they found out they couldn't survive without a flesh body in which to live.

Christ gives us an example of these spirit infested bodies in the book of Matthew,

> And when he was come to the other side into the country of the Gergesenes', there met him two possessed with devils, coming out of the tombs, exceeding fierce, so that no man might pass by that way. And, behold, they cried out, saying, what have we to do with thee, Jesus, thou Son of God? Art, thou come hither to torment us before the time? And there was a good way off from them a herd of many swine feeding. So, the devils besought him, saying, if thou cast us out, suffer us to go away into the herd of swine. And he said unto them "Go". And when they were come out, they went into the herd of swine: and, behold, the whole herd of swine ran violently down a steep place into the sea, and perished in the waters. (Matthew 8:28-32)

We are not told what happened to the devils after the herd of swine perished in the sea-just that they perished. We can conclude though that a spirit must have a flesh body in order to exist in this flesh world. For further emphasis, we have this same story in the book of Mark and in Mark's gospel we find out there are many unclean spirits residing inside this same man who is called "Legion" in this gospel. (Mark 5:1-13)

Because of Satan's introduction of disobedience into God's creation, all will be tried and tested to see who will want to love and obey our Heavenly Father. So now, perhaps you can understand better, the Apostle Paul's dilemma when he cried out,

> O wretched man that I am! Who shall deliver me from the body of this death? (Romans 7:24)

Paul was in turmoil and why not? He believed in the law of God and had tried to live within that law and found the commandants of God only showed him how great his sins were-just as they do to us today. We still have the ten commandants and civil laws to guard our actions. When we break one or the other, the Holy Spirit immediately reminds us of our wrong.

In the first earth age, we didn't have the Holy Spirit to guide us. We knew nothing about sin and its consequences. Everybody loved and obeyed our Heavenly Father, until one man decided he was greater and more powerful than our Father. That man of sin was Satan, the cherub who was there to rule under God and guard God's throne. And as it is written,

> Wherefore, as by one-man sin entered into the world, and death by sin; and so, death passed upon all men, for that all have sinned: (Romans 5:12)

Some teach Adam brought sin into the world by his transgression but the scriptures tell us the 'tree of knowledge of good and evil' was in the Garden of Eden; so for this 'tree' to be there with evil knowledge lets us know sin was already in the world before the creation of Adam. Further as it reads,

> For until the law sin was in the world: but sin is not imputed when there is no law. Nevertheless, death reigned from Adam to Moses, even over them that had not sinned after the similitude of Adam's transgression, who is the figure of him that was to come. (Romans 5:13-14)

As I mentioned, sin was already in the world by Satan's rebellion and the others who chose to exercise their "freedom to choose" began to experiment with little sins. They wanted to know what would happen if they broke a little way from God. It is like a young child who is told not to touch a hot stove because it will burn them. They try to touch it lightly to find out if what you said was true and how much will the burn hurt them. All the sons of God began to want knowledge, and who has access to all this knowledge besides God? You guessed it, Satan. He is the one they turned to for this information. And what did he tell them, "You shall not surely die". The last part is not recorded in the bible, but you can be assured he told them the same thing he told "Eve". So the sentence of death was passed on to all God's creation; now the whole "age" would need something to save it or a "savior" to bring this creation back into good standing with God the Father.

Hence the bible says,

> But not as the offense, so also is the free gift. For if through the offense of one many be dead, much more the grace of God, and the gift by grace, which is by one man, Jesus Christ, hath abounded unto many. And not as it was by one that sinned, so is the gift: for the judgment was by one to condemnation, but the free gift is of many offenses unto justification. (Romans 5:15-16)

Satan committed the first offense and brought about the death penalty for most of the "sons" of God. Only handfuls that trusted our Heavenly Father and never chose to 'sin' and fought against Satan's rebellion have been excluded from this sentence of death. Those who trusted God and honored his commandants have been judged and justified already by God. They are called his elect and are now in this earth age to be used by God to keep this world on the path God wants.

Again, as it is written,

> For if by one man's offence death reigned by one; much more they which receive abundance of grace and of the gift of righteousness shall reign in life by one, Jesus Christ. Therefore, as by the offence of one judgment came upon all men to condemnation; even so by the righteousness of one the free gift came upon all men unto justification of life. For as by one man's disobedience many were made sinners, so by the obedience of one shall many be made righteous. (Romans 5:17-19)

The one man who made the offense was Satan and he caused the death sentence to be passed on all people, animals, and even nature. But Christ came and removed that offense which separates us from our Heavenly Father by paying the debt of with his life. Now all who claim to be servants of Christ are covered with the blood of the righteousness of Christ. And when God looks on our sinful character, he will only see the righteous blood of Christ and our sins are forever hidden. To enter this group under Christ's blood we must acknowledge Jesus as Lord of our life and surrender to his will in our lives. It takes living the rest of this physical life in servitude to his will and daily repentance of our transgressions. You can enter this group so why not do it today?

If you can grasp the truth, that all of the angels who didn't overcome Satan's deceptions, and didn't fight on God's side have to come through this flesh age, we'll get a number of about twelve billion people who have been born of woman. A third of this figure will come to four billion people who fought along side of Satan and against God's followers. Now maybe you can begin to see why God didn't just destroy his children who went astray and were deceived by Satan. Instead, He chose to destroy everything and start over in order to bring as many of his wayward children back to him. In this second earth age, they'll have a chance to decide for themselves who they will love and follow, Satan or God.

Christ touched on this subject when he and Nicodemus were having a conversation, most people in today's world have been misled by uneducated teachers who haven't really studied God's word. The subject is being "born again" and Nicodemus doesn't understand the subject matter. The modern world has the same problem. Most in this modern Christian circle are taught "being born again" is a change of mind and the acceptance of Christ as their savior and Lord. While this is a very good thing, it's not what Christ was referring to at all. Christ was teaching something just as important but few actually understand the words of Christ. Our subject is found in the book of John. Let's look at the actual scripture first. Then I will piece together the symbols and the meaning of Christ's words. The scripture reads,

> There was a man of the Pharisees, named Nicodemus, a ruler of the Jews: the same came to Jesus by night, and said unto him, Rabbi, we know that thou art a teacher come from God: for no man can do these miracles that thou doest, except God be with him. (John 3:1-2)

Why did Nicodemus come at night? Was he concerned the gossips might spread talk of him being a follower of Christ? Maybe Nicodemus just wanted to avoid the crowds? We don't know the reason, but we do know Nicodemus acknowledges Jesus is from God. He just doesn't know Jesus is God. Nicodemus apparently asks a question of Christ which we didn't have in the scriptures, but from the answer Jesus gives, we can guess accurately the subject is whether mankind is only flesh and blood or does a spirit live inside of the flesh body. And if there is a spirit inside the body, what happens at the death of the physical body? Or perhaps, how does a man get to heaven? Christ's answer has been mistranslated in the English King James version, but let's look at the answer Jesus gives Nicodemus and then we'll see what the translation should have been.

> Jesus answered and said unto him, verily, verily, I say unto thee, except a man be born again, he cannot see the kingdom of God. (John 3:3)

The correct translation from the Greek is, "except a man be born from above, he cannot see the kingdom of God." Christ is not discussing somebody being brought into this physical world twice or somebody having a change of mind even though Nicodemus thinks this is the message he receives from Christ. The English word "again" is translated incorrectly from the Greek word "anothen". The correct translation of this word is "from above".

Continuing with the scripture,

Nicodemus saith unto him, how can a man be born when he is old? Can he enter the second time into his mother's womb, and be born? (John 3:4)

Clearly Nicodemus has no understanding of what Jesus is relating to him. He has no idea what being "born from above" means.

In the next verse,

Jesus answered, verily, verily, I say unto thee, except a man be born of water and of the Spirit, he cannot enter into the kingdom of God. (John 3:5)

Some teachers use this verse to teach that all people need to be baptized and receive the Holy Spirit to go to Heaven. This is not what Christ is saying at all. In a nutshell, Christ is telling Nicodemus that God places a spirit of one of his children into every baby at conception, and this spirit is one of his children from the first earth age. The rest of these verses in John will defend what I'm teaching and I'll give you other places where this truth is shown.

The next verses continue Jesus' thoughts,

That which is born of the flesh is flesh; and that which is born of the Spirit is spirit. Marvel not that I said unto thee, ye must be born again. The wind blows where it listeth, and thou hearest the sound thereof, but canst not tell whence it cometh, and whither it goeth: so is every one that is born of the Spirit. (John 3:6-8)

Jesus is explaining flesh brings forth flesh; that is cows bear cows and there isn't a spirit or soul in their flesh bodies. As it is mentioned in the story of the 'Garden of Eden'; God created the man Adam and 'breathed in his nostrils the breath of life and man

(Adam) became a living soul.' (Genesis 2:7) In Nicodemus's case, Jesus went on to explain that mankind as a whole doesn't know which spirit God places into each flesh body. He places whatever pleases Him. This is the symbolism of the wind Jesus gave since the Greek for wind and spirit are the same word.

This knowledge of the spirits being placed into the flesh bodies is important to know because of the "fallen angel offspring" which were born on this earth from flesh women. God refused to place a spirit into these half-breeds. The descendants of Cain fall into this category. (Isaiah 26:13-14)

> Nicodemus answered and said unto him, how can these things be? Jesus answered and said unto him, art that a master of Israel, and knowest not these things? Verily, verily, I say unto thee, we speak that we do know, and testify that we have seen; and ye receive not our witness. If I have told you earthly things, and ye believe not, how shall ye believe, if I tell you of heavenly things? And no man hath ascended up to heaven, but he that came down from heaven, even the Son of man which is in Heaven. (John 3:9-13)

Christ is letting Nicodemus know the spirit returns to God who gave it at the death of the flesh body. (Eccl. 12:7) and unless God places a spirit into a flesh body, there's no spirit to return back to Heaven. Jesus even inferred here that he had the Spirit of God in him and that this spirit came from God. It was placed in him at conception. (Luke 1:41) Elisabeth was six months pregnant when Mary went to see her and the babe in Elisabeth womb leaped at the sound of Mary's voice. Why; because the spirit in Elisabeth's baby recognized the Spirit of God in Mary's baby. So, understand, the spirit is placed at conception.

We have more of what happened in this first earth age given in the book of Jeremiah. In this book, we see God's anger and also his compassion in that he didn't make a full end of his creation. In the fourth chapter of Jeremiah, we will begin our reading with verse nineteen,

> My bowels, my bowels! I am pained at my very heart; my heart maketh a noise in me; I cannot hold my peace, because thou have heard, O my soul, the sound of the trumpet, the alarm of war. (Jeremiah 4:19)

Do you have children which you love dearly? Of course, you have! How do you feel when they squabble and fight amongst themselves? Don't you get angry and try to straighten out the problem? Sure, you do and so did God! He couldn't believe what he was seeing. His children were going to war with each other. What would you have done in God's shoes?

And again, in Jeremiah,

> Destruction upon destruction is cried; for the whole land is spoiled: suddenly are my tents spoiled, and my curtains in a moment. (Jeremiah 4:20)

Can you imagine the vastness of the devastation taking place on the earth at this time? God's children are immortal. All that can happen to them is pain and bruises to self esteem; but everything around this fighting is being torn to smithereens. Remember the destruction of Sodom and Gomorrah we read about in the bible. It took only two angels to make these cities a total ruin.

Continuing with Jeremiah,

> How long shall I see the standard, and hear the sound of the trumpet? For my people are foolish, they have not known me; they are sottish children, and they have no understanding: they are wise to do evil, but to do good they have no knowledge. (Jeremiah 4:21-22)

God wants to know how long this war will last and if his children will ever learn to get along with each other? He calls them "sottish" children; which is an old English word which simply means "stupid". God's children in the first earth age are just like the ones today. We still let the flesh wants and desires take charge of our lives. We still suffer from the influence of pride and vanity. We envy our neighbor's wife, job, car, or anything they have which we think is better than what we have. How true the scripture which states,

> The thing that hath been, it is that which shall be; and that which is done is that which shall be done: and there is no new thing under the sun. (Eccl. 1:9)

Returning to Jeremiah, we read God's judgment being brought about to finish this first earth age. We read,

> I beheld the earth, and lo, it was without form, and void; and the heavens, and they had no light. (Jeremiah 4:23)

What else did God say at this time? Continuing on,

> I beheld, and, lo, there was no man, and all the birds of the heavens were fled. I beheld the mountains, and, lo, they trembled, and all the hills moved lightly. I beheld, and, lo, the fruitful place was a wilderness, and all the cities thereof were broken down at the presence of the Lord, and by his fierce anger. For thus hath

the Lord said, the whole land shall be desolate; yet will I not make a full end. (Jeremiah 4:24-28)

Did you notice, God said there was "no man"? Some teachers have taught these verses are describing Noah's flood; but Noah's flood didn't wipe out all the birds or all the people. These verses above tell us there were no people or birds or cities and everything was desolate. There is no mention of a flood at all, so this can only be talking about the destruction of the first earth age. Perhaps the best thing to determine this scripture's meaning is the statement by God that he wouldn't make a full end. He would give his creation a chance and each child would be given an opportunity to make his or her choice as to whom they would follow.

All of what we've been studying so far has taken place between the first verse and second verse of Genesis, chapter one. Now, you can see why the second verse of Genesis chapter one is correctly translated, "And the earth became without form and void;" God destroyed everything. There was nothing left but a bunch of loose rubble.

Were you able to grasp the full significance of what you just read? God destroyed every living thing: the birds; meaning all flying creatures, and mankind. There was no ark with Noah and a few other people aboard. The plates of the earth were ripped apart and slid asunder. The beautiful earthly paradise God had first created was all gone. Yet God said he wouldn't make a full end. What did he do? He changed his children, all of them, into spirits and ministers of fire. But let God's word tell what took place. And it reads,

Who makes his angels spirits; his ministers a flaming fire: (Psalm 104:4)

Looking back into the book of Jeremiah once again, we read;

For thus the Lord said, the whole land shall be desolate, yet I will not make a full end. For this shall the earth mourn, and the heavens above be black: because I have spoken it. I have purposed it, and will not repent; neither will I turn back from it. (Jeremiah 4:27-28)

As I've stated several times before because I want my readers to fully grasp the significance of what we have read in the Psalms,

Who maketh his angels spirits; his ministers a flaming fire. (Psalm 104:4)

This last statement could be a little hard to understand if we didn't know a little about our Heavenly Father which is given in the book of Hebrews. In Hebrews 12:29 it reads, "For our God is a consuming fire". When we read about his ministers being a "flaming fire", we are to understand the symbolic meaning of the sons of God who fought with God to put Satan's rebellion down, are God servants. These servants of the "Fire" illustrate God as the fire. The rest of his children he just changed into spirit form. These spirits are then placed into newborn babies at the moment of conception. This transaction is what Jesus was teaching Nicodemus when he told Nicodemus he must be born from above. Most King James bibles translate this verse as being born again, but the translation is wrong. Christ went on to say,

> No man hath ascended up to heaven, but he that came down from heaven, even
> the son of man which is in heaven. (John 3:1-13)

The spirit within man can return to heaven because the spirit that dwells in his human body was first from heaven. Likewise, God's spirit that lived within Christ's body could return to heaven because God is spirit and came from heaven. The apostle Peter gives testament to the spirit in his writing where he states,

> Whereby the world (age) that then was, being overflowed with water, perished:
> but the heavens and the earth which are now, by the same word are kept in store,
> reserved unto fire against the day of judgment and perdition of ungodly men. (2
> Peter 3:6-7, emphasis mine)

Do you remember who the fire represents or what the fire is? GOD!

The second part of this second verse in Genesis 1:2 reads, "And darkness was upon the face of the deep". God's not talking about nighttime being brought in. The Hebrew word translated "darkness" in this sentence is "choshek" and literally means: misery, sorrow, dead, destroyed wickedness, and etc. in other words, God killed all life; that is, except his children. (Ps. 104:4) His children were changed into spirits and moved into another dimension or the true place where God dwells. The place Jesus ascended to after his resurrection. The apostle John was given a vision of this place as explained in the book of Revelation. We know this dimension exists because Elisha and his servant were privileged to see into this dimension when an opposing army came to attack them. And God can remove the veil which hides this dimension from our eyes as written in 2 Kings 6:17 any time he so chooses. In this passage, Elisha prayed for God to open his servant's eyes that he might see this into dimension. God's children are kept there until God sends them into this flesh world or age, in the form of a newborn baby. Every spirit which didn't earn or were justified by God in the first earth age has to come through this flesh world, and then, through the Millennium to make up their mind whether they will serve God or Satan. Remember, God is always fair. No one will be sent to Hell or into the Lake of Fire without full knowledge of who God is and what he's all about. Also, his children will know who Satan is and what he's all about. In fact, the type of Hell most preachers and teachers convey to their students doesn't exist at all and never will.

Keep in mind, God is a consuming fire. He's a terror to his enemies and a warming flame to his children whom he loved enough to destroy an entire earth age instead of a third of his children. But if your name isn't written in the "book of Life" you'll be sentenced to die in the Lake of Fire at the Great White Throne Judgment. You can get your name written in the book of life by accepting Jesus Christ as your Lord and Master and living a life Christ with which would be pleased. The "book of life" lists all the things you have every done in this flesh life, but if you have a change of mind or heart and repent of the wrong, the evil you have done is erased. Only the good you have done will remain. Also remember, God is not mocked. He reads minds and emotions and knows the lie from the truth.

Get your act together. There's not much time left for you to decide whether you'll follow Satan or Christ. There's no middle ground.

I might mention here, not all of God's children agreed to this change from a solid body to a spirit body, proposed by God and some changed their minds after the change took place. We'll look into these facets of our story as we go along. I just wanted you to be aware that all was not right in Heaven. Some of the fighting had not completely stopped.

Part Two

The Earth Restored and Blessed:

The last part of verse two reads, "And the Spirit of God moved upon the face of the

waters". (Genesis 1:2) This time period by modern day archeologist would be about three

billion years ago. Surprised? Surely, you didn't believe this planet was only six thousand

years old? Hooray! We finally got through verses one and two of Genesis, and now we'll

pick up with verse three. At this time in history, we have a planet whose surface is

completely covered with water. So, what happens next? "And God said, let there be

light." (Genesis 1:3) The word "light" is translated from the Hebrew word "owr" and

basically means illumination, happiness, bright, and etc. Now if this doesn't fly over your

head, the light was Christ. I know you weren't ready for that piece of knowledge, were

you? Well, just put it on a back shelf, and we'll come back to it later. Just accept the idea

of God bringing "good" into the physical world (age) at this time and calling it "light". It

shouldn't be too hard to grab this concept. Christians are called "children of light". As it

is written in 2 Corinthians,

> In whom the god (Satan) of this world hath blinded the minds of them which
> believe not, lest the light of the glorious gospel of Christ, who is the image of
> God, should shine unto them. (2 Cor. 4:4, parentheses mine)

Paul continues,

> For God, who commanded the light to shine out of darkness, hath shined in our hearts, to give the light of the knowledge of the glory of God in the face of Jesus Christ. (2 Cor. 4:6)

This "light" is not new; it has been with us from the beginning of this physical age. It was the first thing God brought forth in his rejuvenation of this planet after the destruction caused by the rebellion of Satan and his angels as recorded in Genesis,

> And God saw the light, that it was good: and God divided the light from the darkness. (Genesis 1:4)

By calling "light" good, we could infer that darkness is the reverse of light or "evil". People prefer to do their evil work in the darkness. So, darkness is associated with wickedness throughout the bible. This verse is the first mention of Christ or the office Christ will occupy. Because of the rebellion and sin of the angels during the first earth age, there will now have to be a savior to atone for those sins committed in the first earth age. So now we have a division between "good" and "bad". Before the rebellion, there was no darkness only light existed, but now sin has made everything dark and darkness prevailed everywhere. The office of "light" (Christ) would eventually dispel all the darkness, and when sin has been eradicated, only light will be left for all eternity.

Continuing with God's rejuvenation in Genesis,

> And God called the light Day, and the darkness he called Night. And the evening and the morning were the first day. (Genesis 1:5)

Notice, God's time period starts at sundown and the first part of the time period is called night. This is symbolic of sin being in the world before Christ came to get rid of the evil or darkness. The "Light" or "day" comes after night and is there to dispel sinful things. How long was this first day measured by our standards? Nobody knows for sure; maybe a thousand years or a million. It was whatever length of time God used to get this part of his job done.

In the next verse of Genesis,

> God said, let there be a firmament in the midst of the waters, and let it divide the waters from the waters. (Genesis 1:6)

The word firmament is translated from the Hebrew word "raqiya" and means literally an "expanse" or in this sense, a visible arch of the sky. Picture in your mind a planet similar to the planet Venus. Like Venus this planet is shrouded in vapor and thick clouds of moisture with the surface completely covered with water. Now, visualize a large balloon being placed around the globe of this planet and something starts to fill the balloon with air. As it increases in size all the clouds and vapor were pushed by the balloon to several miles away from the planet. With this imaginary in mind, we can readily see the meaning of "let it divide the waters from the waters" as stated above. As we continue our study in Genesis, we can visualize this action as it takes place in the next verse:

> And God made the firmament and divided the waters which were under the firmament (the water covered earth) from the waters which were above the firmament; (high clouds and vapor; which acted like a large ozone layer protecting the earth) and it was so. (Genesis 1:7, parentheses mine)

The bible tells us he did this on the second day. God called this firmament "Heaven" in the sense that it was higher than mankind could reach as his ways are higher than our ways. Verses nine through nineteen are fairly self-explanatory and no reason to spend time going over something you already know, but when we look at verse twenty, there's a little something which needs to be pointed out for your consideration. Verse twenty reads,

> And God said let the waters bring forth abundantly the moving creature that hath life, and fowl that may fly above the earth in the open firmament of heaven. (Genesis 1:20)

The word or subject we are concerned with is "life". It comes from the Hebrew word "chay" and means "alive; life". Notice, the scripture stated the "waters" were to bring forth abundantly a creature which "hath life". It didn't say to bring forth a creature and life would be placed into it. What the waters were to bring forth already had LIFE. This just goes to show the evolutionist theory of how life started on this planet and the way it really happened are not very far apart. God doesn't bother telling us how he did it-just that he did it. The evolutionist are more interested in the way life was brought about. Of course, evolution needs a catalyst for their primeval soup mixture to work; God says he is that catalyst. (Isaiah 45:12)

It is in the next verse of Genesis, verse twenty-one, where it states,

> And God created great whales, (fish) and every living creature that moveth, which the waters brought forth abundantly, after their kind, and every winged fowl after his kind: and God saw that it was good. (Genesis 1:21)

Next, we have the animals living on dry land or air breathing animals brought into existence. It seems to me this is the same way evolutionist claim the earth became populated by fish moving or crawling out of the water to dry land. These creatures only stayed short periods of time at first, but gradually stayed longer and longer as their lungs developed to breathe air. And then finally after many millions of years or on God's sixth day:

> And God said; let us make man in our image, after our likeness: and let them have dominion over the fish of the sea and over the fowl of the air, and over the cattle, and over all the earth, and over every creeping thing that creepeth upon the earth. (Genesis 1:26)

Again, this seems to me to be what archeologist claim has happened and also the evolutionist paint their stories the same way. What is so amazing is that a man named Moses had all this written down. How could he know, unless some superior intellect or maybe God told him what to write? His writings have been studied for the next six thousand years; give or take a few years more or less.

Did you notice the little word "us" written above? Who was God talking to when he said let "us"? Could he have been talking to his children who had not followed Satan? In other words, the angels who are still doing the Father's will. How long did God spend bringing mankind onto the earth? I don't know. The bible gives a day; but a day with God is as a thousand years of our time. Notice again, I said as a thousand; not exactly a thousand years, but "as" a thousand years. The intent of the scriptures, I believe, is to convey the idea of whatever time God decided to use is the amount of time it took. It could have been two hundred thousand years or over a million years. We know from examples given in the bible that God does things most of the time by natural means.

After mankind has been brought forth on the earth, God gave them a job to do and an occupation. When I say "occupation", I mean the type of work they were to do to keep their flesh bodies alive. What were they to do? They were to "replenish" the earth and "subdue" it. God commanded his newly formed mankind to "replenish" the earth. If you are to replenish something, there had to have been something before for you to replenish it. Meaning, the earth had been full of people at one time; that is if you consider angels as men as God does. These people were removed from earth and changed into spirits; (Psalm 104:4) this is the reason God commanded this new creation to "replenish" the earth. They were to eat fruit and nuts to stay alive. There's no mention of killing wild game for food. And also, the beasts of the earth were vegetarians at this time in history. (Genesis 1:26-31)

After this is all in place, God rested or took a break. The bible tells us he rested on the seventh day. We know from our studies above, a thousand years are as one day with God. So the interval between when God finished "renewing" the earth and to his next big project was a thousand years or more. It could have been one hundred thousand years of our time.

The next project God brings upon the stage of the world is a different sort of man. A man created by God and whose descendants would ultimately be the ones who would birth this living God into a flesh world. It had to be a pure line because God is pure. This man was called "Adam" in the English translation, but in Hebrew manuscripts, this man is called "eth-Haadham". (Genesis 2:7) This Hebrew word translates into English as "the man Adam". This is a different creation than the first Adam created in Genesis 1:26-27 and happened at a much later date.

The bible tells us God put a deep sleep on this man Adam. God opened a side up and took a rib and formed woman. This part isn't right either. The actual scriptures say God put the man Adam in a deep sleep and a curve was taken out. I guess the original translators could only visualize a curve as being a rib bone. But now days, we are familiar with the DNA modular and the Helix curve, so we can easily see God took out the female attributes from Adam and made a female from it. This female was named Eve and called "woman" because she was taken out of man. Eve had twin sons born and named them Cain and Abel. They didn't get along and finally in anger, Cain murdered Abel. This act of murder got God's attention, and he faced Cain with his deed. Cain was banished from the area of his birth by God. He traveled eastward and took a wife in the land of Nod and lived there. As the bible records it,

> And Cain went out from the presence of the Lord, and dwelt in the land of Nod, on the east of Eden. And Cain knew his wife; and she conceived, and bare Enoch: and he built a city, and called the name of the city, after the name of his son, Enoch. (Genesis 4:16-17)

If you had a little trouble accepting the fact other races of people were created before Adam and Eve, this should convince you they existed. Otherwise, there wouldn't have been people living east of Eden for Cain to find a wife among them.

I know, I know, the bible informs us that "Eve" is the mother of all living. (Genesis 3:20) But what you haven't grasped is that all life is in Christ, and if you are not in Christ you are not living. Stay with me now, we are talking about the real you. Your spirit is what is the real you and has been living from the first creation which took place millions of years ago until present. Because of the rebellion of Satan and his followers, God's children have been put under a death sentence. Only the angels who activity fought against Satan are exempt from this death warrant. Rebellion against God breaks the first commandant and therefore is "sin". We learn in the book of Hebrews, there's no remission of sin without the shedding of blood. (Hebrews 9:22) Christ's blood on the cross paid the "sin debt" and to enter heaven or the kingdom of God has to be through Christ. In other words, Christ has to vouch for you as one of his followers. You can get this pass or voucher by placing your trust and faith in Christ's ability to defeat death. Death has many forms. The death of the flesh body is a form of death of which we are all familiar. Christ shows he has authority over this type of death when he raised the twelve year old girl back to physical life as stated in Luke 8:51 through 8:55. Because some might not believe the girl was really dead physically but was just in a "coma", Jesus

commanded Lazarus to "come forth" after he had been in the tomb for four days and

nights. Jesus waited this long to prove his mastery over death of the flesh. (John 11:1-44)

Then there is the death of the spirit which is a different facet altogether. Death of the

spirit is the total eraser of your total existence. It means the blotting out of everything

which even faintly refers to your every having been a presence, memory, or thought. It is

as if you never existed in this second earth age or the first earth age. God tells us,

> And fear not them which kill the body, but are not able to kill the soul: but rather
> fear him which is able to destroy both soul and body in hell. (Matt. 10:28)

God is the only entity who can destroy your total presence. In addition to these types

of "death", there is Satan who is called "Death" It is one of his names or "titles" as

recorded in Revelation,

> And I looked, and behold a pale horse: and his name that sat on him was Death,
> and Hell followed with him. And power was given unto them over the fourth part
> of the earth, to kill with sword, and with hunger, and with death, and with the
> beasts of the earth. (Rev. 6:8)

This "Death" is the person Christ came into this age to defeat and to destroy. Some

people refer to him as the "grim reaper" or the "death angel", but regardless of the name

you know him by, he still brings fear and sadness to your lives. In Hebrews we read,

> Forasmuch then as the children are partakers of flesh and blood, he also himself
> likewise took part of the same; that through death he might destroy him that had
> the power of death, that is, the devil; and deliver them who through fear of death
> were all their lifetime subject to bondage. (Hebrews 2:14-15)

We will all suffer the death of the flesh unless Christ returns before the flesh body wears out and dies. But to escape the second death or a spiritual death requires you to believe in Christ and then accept him as your Lord. If you do this, then he will provide you with a new spiritual body upon his return to earth. This new body won't wear out and will be used to house your real self instead of this temporary flesh you are using at present. Christ won't do this for you unless you change your ways and repent of the wrong you have done in your life. One thing to remember, Christ reads minds, so there's no way to fool him into believing you have changed. You have to really change and support his kingdom. There's no free ride. So, in essence, umbilical cord to umbilical cord, Eve is the mother of Christ and only in Christ can you have life. This reason and this reason only is why Eve is called the mother of all living.

Satan Enters and the Consequence:

59

Well, I guess you thought we would be through with Satan; after all, he and his cohorts were defeated and surely God would just destroy the evil doer. Not so, this wasn't about a handful of people gone wrong. This was about a great many of God's children gone bad or deceived into thinking Satan's way was the best way. We still have this thinking in the world today. Perhaps you don't realize how many of God's children turned against the Father. Judging by today's population and the amount of people who have already passed thru this physical world, I would say the number of children who followed Satan in the rebellion would be several billion. And that's not all, besides the ones who rebelled there are the "fence straddlers". I label "fence straddlers" as the ones who could care less about who did what. They just want to be left alone to do "their thing". Look around, we still have them with us today. So, you see God chose to destroy everything except his children. He would start over. He would bring his children through a flesh age and let them make up their minds as to whose life style they would follow. If they chose Satan, God would destroy them with Satan. But if they realized they had been conned and repented, and choose to follow Christ, he would forgive them their sins and accept them into his kingdom.

So now you see what is at stake, we have a war on our hands. If Christ wins, God gets his children back; if Satan wins, everybody loses because God will destroy everything once again and start over. Satan thinks he can win this war and God won't have the heart to destroy all his children. God didn't the first time and Satan believes he won't the second time, but he's wrong on all accounts. As powerful as Satan is, he can only do what God allows him to do. Now, with this thought in mind, let's take a look in the "Garden of Eden" and see what's taking place there.

In chapter three of the book of Genesis, we find the serpent and Eve talking. Satan is questioning Eve concerning the commandant God gave to Adam. Just because God gave the instruction to Adam doesn't relieve Eve of her responsibility in carrying out the commandant. Satan approached Eve because he figured she might be easier to persuade that God was not serious in his orders to Adam. Nothing has changed; a male salesperson will not get the time of day unless he is selling something I want. But a nice female saleslady can have my attention for hours on end to peddle her product. And Satan was the best-looking thing in the Garden; also, God had not spoken to her directly and her knowledge of the commandant not to eat of the tree of knowledge of good and evil had only come thru Adam. Nevertheless, listen to their conversation: Satan speaking first and saying,

Yea, hath God said, ye shall not eat of every tree of the garden? (Genesis 3:1)

And the woman said unto the serpent, we may eat of the fruit of the trees of the garden: but of the fruit of the tree which is in the midst of the garden, God hath said, ye shall not eat of it, neither shall ye touch it, lest ye die. (Genesis 3:2)

And the serpent said unto the woman, ye shall not surely die: for God doth know that in the day ye eat thereof, then your eyes shall be opened, and ye shall be as gods, knowing good and evil. (Genesis 3:4-5)

This example of how sin entered God's new renewed "Garden" is the same for every individual since that fateful day. Our eyes and ears see and hear things that our mind thinks it wants. We forget the rules God laid down for us to live by. We rationalize the sin part out of our lives and forget God said "No". We sin just like Eve did, and we think its not a great sin if other people are doing it too. As Eve led Adam into her sin, we let others make us a party to their sin. It doesn't change our guilt and Satan goes his merry way laughing at God.

Later, Adam and Eve heard God calling for them and because of sin now in their lives, they hid from God. Let's listen in again on the actual scene as it unfolds; and the Lord God called unto Adam, and said unto him,

Where are thou? (Genesis 3:9)

And He said, I heard thy voice in the garden, and I was afraid, because I was naked; and I hid myself. (Genesis 3:10)

And He said, "Who told thee that thou wast naked? Hast thou eaten of the tree, whereof I commanded thee that thou shouldest not eat? (Genesis 3:11)

And the man said, the woman whom thou gavest to be with me, she gave me of the tree, and I did eat. (Genesis 3:12)

Just like a man; always ready to blame somebody else when they are caught with their hand in the cookie jar. In this case, Adam blamed Eve for disobeying God.

> And the Lord God said unto the woman, what is this that thou hast done? (Genesis 3:13)

> And the woman said, the serpent beguiled me, and I did eat. Genesis (3:13)

Eve admitted to her guilt and stood ready to face the consequences for her part in this sin of disobedience to God. Next, God turned to the serpent:

> And the Lord God said unto the serpent, because thou hast done this, thou art cursed above all cattle, and above every beast of the field; upon thy belly shalt thou go, and dust shalt thou eat all the days of thy life; and I will put enmity between thee and the woman, and between thy seed and her seed; it shall bruise thy head, and thou shalt bruise His heel. (Genesis 3:14-15)

All right, we're going to have to spend some time on these passages to get a full understanding of what has happened and the implications of God's judgment. We will begin with the word "Eden" and the true meaning of the scriptures. The word Eden from the root Hebrew word "adan" means, "be soft" or "pleasant" and also, figuratively to live "voluptuously". So, was "Eden" a place to live or a way of life? The thought sounds "heavenly" doesn't it; and perhaps it was. I've always been intrigued about why the bible states "God planted a garden eastward in Eden? Why didn't he plant the garden northward or southward or westward; and also, eastward of what? A bit confusing, isn't it? And then there is the "ground" which grew all the trees; what kind of ground could that be? The Hebrew word translated "ground" is "adamah" and ground is one of the meanings; also, it means country, earth, land, and husband. How about that; you would never have guessed husband could have been used in the translation of this sentence of the bible. How about we go a little deeper in what's happening here in the "garden". We have in the garden two adults, a man and a woman who are as innocent as two new born babies except they have adult bodies and a thirst for knowing the unknown. God the "husband" or "ground" has brought forth instructors (trees) for their learning (food) of his kingdom and a test to see if they would love him and obey him. This test was in the form of a very beautiful tree (Satan); it had a lot of knowledge (food) about all kinds of things. But, God had forbidden them to learn (touch) from this tree. God had told them not to touch it or they would die. This word "touch" is translated from the Hebrew word "naga" and literary means to "lie with a woman" in a sexual capacity.

One of the trees in this garden was the tree of life, it says and one of the others was the tree of knowledge of good and evil we mentioned above. (Genesis 2:9) Of the different trees in the garden, we know the tree of life was the living Christ. (Rev. 22:2 and Luke 23:31) And the tree of knowledge of good and evil was the serpent or Satan. How about that, the leader of the rebellion situated here in this garden of plenty. It's no wonder, God told Adam not to have anything to do with this tree. But he did; he was introduced to the serpent by his wife Eve and both were seduced by the evil one.

When questioned by God, Adam blamed Eve for his undoing; Eve admitted her guilt and told the Lord, "The serpent beguiled (seduced) me". The Lord didn't question the serpent; Satan knew what he was doing and his planned worked. He had won the first battle on God's renewed earth. Satan had brought sin into this new world God had just finished overhauling from the destruction caused by the rebellion of the Deceiver and his cohorts. Because of that rebellion in the first earth age, the sinful children (angels) needed a way to be reconciled back to the Father. And now, since this renewed earth had just been contaminated by Satan in the Garden of Eden, it also needed a savior too. What was God to do now? As it is written in the book of Hebrews, "And almost all things are by law purged with blood; and without the shedding of blood, there is no remission". (Heb. 9:22) Later on in this age, God would shed his own blood in the form of Jesus and become this sacrifice God would require of mankind to be reconciled back to the Father in good standing. .

Because of what he had done, God only told Satan what would be his end result. The woman would be pregnant with twins; one would be Satan's child, Cain and one would be Adam's child, Abel. (Genesis 4:1-2) Some people believe erroneously Adam and Eve to be the first humans God created in this renewed earth because it says in the bible, "And Adam called his wife's name Eve; because she was the mother of all living". (Genesis 3:20) The reason Eve is called the "mother of all living" is simply because umbilical cord to umbilical cord, she is the mother of Jesus Christ. It is only in Christ that you can have life and without Christ, you are a dead man walking. (Col. 1:13-22) I know I've stated this before, but I'm giving it to you again to make sure this truth is imprinted in your mind.

Eve was pregnant and gave birth to twins: we find written,

> And Adam knew his wife; and she conceived, and bare Cain, and said I have gotten a man from the Lord. And she again bare his brother Abel. And Abel was a keeper of sheep, but Cain was a tiller of the ground. (Genesis 4:1-2)

Most bible readers understand Cain and Abel were brothers but didn't know they were twins by two different fathers. The word, "again" in the phrase given above, "and she again bare his brother" is translated incorrectly for this subject. The Hebrew word is "yacaph" and means to "add to" or "augment" and "to continue to do a thing"; as in this case it means to continue in labor to birth another child. This child was Abel. You don't believe me, do you? Alright, check out Genesis, chapter four; here you'll find Cain's descendents listed and Adam is not mentioned. And if you'll read chapter five of Genesis, you'll learn of Adam's descendents and Cain is not mentioned. Also, look in the New Testament where Jesus is addressing some Jews who claim to be descendents of Judah, one of Jacob's sons from Isaac and Christ tells them who they are really descended from.

We read,

> I speak that which I have seen with my Father: and ye do that which ye have seen with your father. (John 8:38)

In this sentence alone, Christ is showing the ones he was conversing with have a different ancestor then he does. Of course, they disagree and argue the point.

They answered and said unto him, Abraham is our father. (John 8:39)

They are claiming to de descendants of Judah and also have the heritage of Abraham. Do you know why they would claim to be Abraham's kin? The promises God made were to Abraham and to his prodigy and this bunch was trying to claim an inheritance that wasn't theirs.

Jesus saith unto them, if ye were Abraham's children, ye would do the works of Abraham. But ye seek to kill me, a man that hath told you the truth, which I heard of God: this did not Abraham. Ye do the deeds of your father. (John 8:30-41)

What are the deeds of their father? Christ will lay it out for them before he's through talking.

They said unto him, we be not born of fornication; we have one father, even God. (John 8:41)

Jesus said unto them, if God were your Father, ye would love me: for I proceeded forth and came from God; neither came I of myself, but he sent me. Why do ye not understand my speech; even because ye cannot hear my word? Ye are of your father the devil, and the lusts of your father ye will do. He was a murderer from the beginning, and abode not in the truth, because there is no truth in him. When he speaketh a lie, he speaketh of his own: for he is a liar, and the father of it. (John 8:44)

Who was the first murderer? It was Cain, of course. These people claiming to be Jews are in fact Kenites. In the book of Revelation, Christ commends the two churches who teach the truth about the Kenites. Our scripture reads,

> Behold, I will make them of the synagogue of Satan, which say they are Jews, and are not, but do lie; behold, I will make them to come and worship before thy feet, and to know that I have loved thee. (Rev. 3:9)

These verses which are given above show Satan has physical offspring or children on this planet. And, for more proof, if we turn in the bible to chapter three of the book of first John, we read,

> Not of Cain, who was of that wicked one, and slew his brother. And wherefore slew he him? Because his own works were evil, and his brother's righteous. (1 John 3:12)

Who is this wicked one John speaking of? There is only one entity in the bible constantly referred to as "the wicked one" and that person is Satan.

Mankind dealt with as a whole:

For the next several hundred years we see the offspring of Cain spreading over the world and the children of Adam multiplying and spreading over the land. We are not told but also the children of the sixth day creation are also multiplying and spreading over the land. Most of the time, these peoples are referred to as "the strangers" in your midst; until we finally come to Noah and his children. We are given the pedigree of Adam all the way down the family tree to Noah to prove there is an unblemished bloodline from Adam to Noah. The bible calls Noah perfect, but this doesn't mean Noah is not sinful; it means no part of his family tree has married outside the Adamic bloodline. This is important because the Christ is to come from this Adamic bloodline and there can't be any outside blood of another race mixed with it. Satan knows what God plans to do and he'll try anything to keep Christ from being born into this sinful flesh world of which he is the ruler at present.

How can Satan be the ruler of this present world? Simply, God won't have anything to do with sin and a sinful world is not something he will come into contact with, Oh yes, he'll keep it chartered on a course which pleases him, but he'll do this through human effort. He'll work thru people like Noah, Abraham, Moses, David, Cyrus, Jesus, and etc. I think you get my meaning. Satan sees his job is to pollute this link to Adam and thus keep the Christ from ever being born. This way, he will be able to rule this planet for ever.

So in chapter 6 of the book of Genesis, we find Satan once again trying to pollute Adam's bloodline. And we read,

> And it came to pass, when men began to multiply on the face of the earth, and daughters were born unto them, that the sons of God saw the daughters of men that they were fair; and they took them wives of all which they chose. (Genesis 6:1-2)

The "sons of God" mentioned here are some of the fallen angels who followed Satan in the rebellion of the 1st earth age. The idea conceived by Satan was to mix their "fallen angel" blood with all the Adamic women living on earth, and therefore prevent God from using any of this line of women on the earth to be the mother of the Christ. As we are reading about Noah, we see his plan almost succeeded because only Noah and his family carried a pure bloodline back to Adam.

The rest of the families on earth had married outside of their clan and no longer could claim pure Adamic Blood in their veins. Some had bred with the children of the sixth day creation, but most had been seduced by the 'fallen angels' led by Satan. This mixed marriage produced strange results; some of the children were giants, some were grossly deformed and were most likely the seed for the mythological creatures passed down in storytelling through the centuries.

Let's continue,

> And the Lord said, my spirit shall not always strive with man, for that he is also
> flesh: yet his days shall be an hundred and twenty years. (Genesis 6:3)

The word "strive" may give you a little trouble. It comes from the Hebrew word "diyn" and literally means "to rule"; but expresses the thought of God directing or contending man's life. But regardless of his lifestyle, unless he is taken out by an accident or is killed in some fashion, God has degreed his life span to be 120 years. Before this decree by God, mankind was living six or seven hundred years. According to the bible, Methuselah is said to have lived nine hundred sixty-nine years. Later on as mankind multiplied on earth, God would again change the lifespan of mankind. God would shorten his lifespan to seventy years and if he pleased God an additional ten years could be given.

Next, we find,

> There were Giants in the earth in those days: and also after that, when the sons of
> God came in unto the daughters of men, and they bare children to them, the same
> became mighty men which were of old, men of renown. (Genesis 6:4)

To get an understanding of what has taken place, we have to look up the word "giants" from the Hebrew. The Hebrew word is "nephyial" and is a derivative of the root work "napal", which means to fall or fallen. We are to understand these "giants" were the results of fallen angels (sons of God) producing children from human women; that is the daughters of Adam, and these giants were a bad lot. They took what they wanted from whomever they met and kept the human population under their control. This is what the phrase "the same became mighty men which were of old, men of renown". (Genesis 6:4) Some of the ancient Greek myths and legends were probably passed down thru the generations from this mating of the "angels".

> And God saw that the wickedness of man was great in the earth, and that every imagination of the thoughts of his heart was only evil continually. (Genesis 6:5)

Some teachers teach the descendants of Adam had become sinful; not so, only the children of the fallen angels and the children of the giants were the ones God was describing. The only problem was that besides Noah and his family, there were no pure descendants of Adam left. Satan has almost won another battle in his continual war with God. He knows that if he can pollute all the living offspring of Adam which are on this earth, he wins, because there's no way for Christ to enter this age in the flesh through a descendant of Adam. The situation had become very grave. This is the reason God declares,

> And it repented the Lord that he had made man on the earth and it grieved him at his heart. (Genesis 6:6)

For mankind to be in the flesh was not a good thing; the flesh created too many desires and with the brain given to mankind, there wasn't a lot he couldn't accomplish in this world. Proof of my statement; just look around you, see the physical marvels mankind has produced. But what about the man inside these flesh bodies; the spiritual man, the true person, what has happened to him? The physical man is just too busy for

God to speak to him. I'm talking about the real man inside the flesh; or is that just my opinion?

What was God to do? It was time for drastic action, so God decided to destroy all life from the face of the earth once more and start over. But there was one family who had not mixed with the fallen angels or their offspring. As the bible reads,

> And the Lord said, I will destroy man whom I have created from the face of the earth; both man, and beast, and the creeping thing, and the fowls of the air; for it repented me that I have made them. But Noah found grace in the eyes of the Lord. (Genesis 6:7-8)

Do you see what one person or one family can do when they trust God to work through them?

Most all of us know the story of Noah and the flood. We know the Lord told Noah to build an ark and to save a male and female from all the species to repopulate the earth after the flood was over and the waters had receded back into their natural borders. Into the ark was placed seven of the clean beast and two of the unclean beasts. Also, what a lot of people miss is that the Lord told Noah to take on the ark besides his sons and their wives and Noah's wife, a pair of the different races living on the earth at this time. (Genesis 1:26-27) As it reads,

> And of every living thing of all flesh, two of every sort shall thou bring into the ark, to keep them alive with thee; they shall be male and female. (Genesis6:19)

And again,

> And they went in unto Noah into the ark, two and two of all flesh, wherein is the breath of life. And they that went in went in male and female of all flesh, as the God had commanded him: and the Lord shut him in. (Genesis 6:15-16)

You didn't read over the part where it said "two of all flesh" did you. Humans are flesh and were paired up, male and female. But the hybrids were not chosen because they were not pure humans and were sired by the fallen angels. So, we can deduce we had two black people, male and female; two yellow people, male and female; and two white people, male and female; plus two Kenites (children of Cain), male and female; that is unless they were considered the two white people. Common sense agrees with what I'm stating because you can look around you and see; they are still with us. The Kenites making it through the flood are easy to check out; they are mentioned again in the book of Judges and again in 1 Chronicles 2:55. I suppose the Kenites had been around for so many centuries and mixed with humans until they were considered as human.

To really grasp what has taken place, we need to keep in mind what the object of the flood was. God wanted to get rid of the hybrids roaming the earth from the fallen angel mating with human women. He wasn't angry with the humans he had created. He was just angry with Satan and his bunch for trying to ruin his plan to reconcile his wayward children back to him. He didn't want his new creation to know what had happened in the first earth age and the mess Satan had generated. He wanted them to come through this flesh age innocent of the previous age and give them a fair opportunity to decide who they would follow, God or Satan. But as usual, Satan doesn't play fair; and he never will. Just something for you to remember as you continue reading and living your life.

Anyway, God loaded up the ark with the ones who were supposed to survive the next step in God's plan. The next step was to flood the whole earth and destroy all the hybrids the fallen angels had created by their mating. God would start over in his quest to give his wayward children a chance to change and accept him and his way of doing things.

After the flood, we have Noah and his three sons who are of Adamic descent; so God just steps back in the shadows so to speak and lets his small family grow. We are not told, but my guess is that this time was spent by God's obedient angels chasing down and chaining up as many fallen angels as they could lay their hands on. We do have a mention of them in the book of Jude. There we read,

> And the angels who kept not their first estate, but left their own habitation, he hath reserved in everlasting chains under darkness unto the judgment of the great day. (Jude 1:6)

The next several hundred years are spent repopulating the earth with the various tribes settling in different parts and staking a claim to where they located themselves.

Of Noah's three sons, Ham, Seth, and Japheth; Ham and his line became disqualified soon after the flood. Ham found his father and mother drunk from new wine and while his father was passed out from drink, Ham seduced his mother and Canaan was born from this union. Later in the scriptures, we learn Ham mixed with the peoples of Africa and the Egyptians were the results.

Some people think the black man came from this union between Ham and his mother, they teach God cursed Canaan and turned him black. This story is wrong on all points; first God didn't curse Canaan, Noah cursed Canaan when he found out what happened while he was passed out drunk. Let's read what the bible tells us,

> And Noah began to be a husbandman, and he planted a vineyard: and he drank of the wine, and was drunk; and he was uncovered within his tent. And Ham, the father of Canaan, saw the nakedness of his father, and told his two brethren without. And Shem and Japheth took a garment, and laid it upon both their shoulders, and went backward, and covered the nakedness of their father; and their faces were backward, and they saw not their father's nakedness. And Noah awoke from his wine, and knew what his younger son had done unto him. And he said cursed be Canaan; a servant of servants shall he be unto his brethren. (Genesis 9:20-25)

Now then, do you really think a son looking on his father's old naked body would warrant a curse? But you say; it says right there in the bible, Ham saw his father's nakedness and Noah cursed Canaan because Ham saw his father naked. And you're right, that's what the bible tells us; but ask yourself, if Ham saw this unpardonable sight of his father's old naked body, why did Noah curse Canaan? Canaan wasn't even born at this time.

So, you see, something is not quite right here; and when you see something in the bible which doesn't gee-haw or make sense, do a little research into the original language of which this part of the bible was translated. If the translation is correct, search the bible and find other cases of the same subject. In our case with the "nakedness" of Noah, we find our answer in the book of Leviticus in the part dealing with the laws of sexual morality, and we read,

> None of you shall approach to any that is near of kin to him, to uncover their nakedness: I am the Lord, the nakedness of thy father, or the nakedness of thy mother, shall thou not uncover: she is thy mother; thou shall not uncover her nakedness. The nakedness of thy father's wife shall thou not uncover: it is thy father's nakedness. (Leviticus 18:6-8)

And again,

> And the man that lies with his father's wife hath uncovered his father's nakedness: both of them shall surely be put to death; their blood shall be upon them. (Leviticus 20:11)

Read all these complete chapters to get a good view of the way God looks on sexual acts and what he approves and what he doesn't approve.

Ok, what did you get from the scriptures? You should have gotten an understanding of what took place between Ham and his father and mother. But if you didn't, I'll spell it out for you. Ham found his parents drunk and naked and Ham went in to his mother's bed and had sex with her. The result was the child Canaan was born. When Noah found out, he cursed Canaan because he was born of this sinful union. God didn't curse Canaan; in fact, Canaan made quite a name for himself. But the name he made wasn't pleasing to God.

And while we are on the subject of Canaan, let's take a look at another offspring of Ham. His grandson Nimrod by Cush started the first known world empire. As it reads in Genesis,

> And Cush begat Nimrod: he began to be a mighty one in the earth. He was a mighty hunter before the Lord: wherefore it is said, even as Nimrod the mighty hunter before the lord. And the beginning of his kingdom was Babel, and Erech, and Accad, and Calneh, in the land of Shinar. (Genesis 10:8-10)

Nimrod is given credit for starting the first known world empire. Ancient history also credits the name Nimrod as being Gilgamesh, Amraphel, and Hammurabi in the legends of pagan creation. Most historians credit Nimrod with being born about two hundred and fifty years after the flood of Noah's day. Nimrod was a powerful man and defeated all who opposed him; he fought and won a great victory against the sons of Ham and the sons of Japhet when he was in his forties. After this war, he built the city of Shinar and ruled from this place. It was while Nimrod was ruling in Shinar, historians claim Abraham was born.

Nimrod's empire became very powerful, and with Chedorlaomer and the kings who sided with them, conquered all of what is now called 'the middle east' and killed the giants living in the area. This destruction of the fallen angel children was probably one of the reasons Nimrod was called the 'mighty hunter before God' in the Genesis account.

Legend tells us Nimrod trusted in only himself to defeat his enemies and mistrusted the Living God because he blamed God for having killed all his forefathers in the flood of

Noah's day. Because of this distrust, Nimrod turned his government of his people into a dictatorship and introduced the worship of the stars by providing his people with twelve wood carvings portraying the twelve months of the year of which are called the signs of the Zodiac. He instructed his people to worship a different god each month as this god's time came about. In his remembrance of the great flood, Nimrod commanded his people to build a tower so high God couldn't destroy all mankind again with another flood. This he did about three hundred and thirty-seven years after the flood of Noah's time with which God used to cover the earth. This tower Nimrod had built was called the "Tower of Babel" because it was at this time God confused the language of the people. "Babel" translated from the Hebrew means "confusion".

There was another war between Hams descendants and Chedorlaomer about three hundred and forty years from Noah's time in which Sodom, Gomorrah, and other cities were conquered and began to pay tribute to Chedorlaomer for the next twelve years, and then they rebelled again. History again claims Nimrod was at the head of this rebellion and his cities remained free for five years. This freedom gave Nimrod the notion of believing Chedorlaomer was weak and Nimrod attacked the Elamite Empire in Persia. In this war with Chedorlaomer, Nimrod's son Mardon was killed and Nimrod was defeated.

This Mardon was supposedly more wicked then his father and is the one whose mother, Semiramis, claims was killed by a wild boar and later resurrected into a god. This is the same personage called Tammuz in the bible as stated in Ezekiel 8:14-16.

The loss of this war put Nimrod back into subjection to Chedorlaomer; Chedorlaomer's victory caused the kings of Goyim and Elasar to make a covenant with Chedorlaomer. This was fruitful, for Nimrod again rebelled and caused Chedorlaomer to attack this area with his coalition of kings. This happened three hundred and seventy-eight years from the date of Noah's flood and is the same story told in the bible where Abraham's nephew Lot is captured. This capture of Lot caused Abraham with the help of three hundred and eighteen soldiers bred in his own household to follow Chedorlaomer and defeat him and rescue his nephew Lot. It was at this time Abraham met Melchizedek, King of Salem, and gave him tithes of all he plundered from rescuing Lot. It is evident from his actions; Abraham recognized his victory was accomplished only by the help or intervention of our Heavenly Father.

As time marched on, the cities of Sodom and Gomorrah continued to increase in wickedness until God would take it no more. And three hundred and ninety-one years after the flood of Noah, God destroyed all the cities of the plains including Sodom and Gomorrah with only Lot and his two daughters being spared. We are told by historians that four hundred and sixty-seven years after the flood of Noah's time, Nimrod was beheaded by Esau and he was buried in his city. After Nimrod's death, his cities were divided into many divisions and other kings took over their rule. All the families descended from Nimrod were enslaved to all the other kings of the area. So ends the saga of Nimrod, the mighty hunter before God; or as a modern translation of these verses from

Genesis, "Cush begat Nimrod; he began to be a tyrant in the earth. He was a tyrannical hunter in opposition to the Lord. Thus, it is said, 'Nimrod the tyrannical opponent of YHVH'. (Genesis 10:8-9)

The above article about Nimrod is compiled from the book of Jasper 7:27; the book of Josephus Antiquities one 4:2-9; King James Bible, Genesis 10:8-11.

The Chosen Nation Called and Blessed:

From the eleventh chapter of Genesis to the end of Malachi we see God using a different approach to provide a way for him to enter this age in the flesh. Eventually, God chose a descendent of Noah thru his son Shem's bloodline. The man was Abram and lived in Haran at the time God spoke to him. Abram's father, Terah had just died being two hundred and five years in age and God chose this time to separate Abram from his people. He told Abram,

> Get thee out of thy country, and from thy kindred, and from thy father's house, unto a land that I will shew thee: and I will make of thee a great nation, and I will bless thee, and make thy name great; and thou shall be a blessing: and I will bless them that bless thee, and curse him that curseth thee: and in thee shall all families of the earth be blessed. (Genesis 12:1-3)

Did you know, from Abraham's loins, we have the real Nation of Israel living in Europe, Soviet Union, the Americas, and Australia, plus parts of Africa and Asia. God is pretty good at keeping his promises, isn't he? And O' yes, I didn't forget; but all the Arabic nations are descended from Abraham, including Iran and surrounding areas through Abraham's second wife Keturah's sons, Zimran, Jokshan, Medan, Midian, Ishbak, and Shuah. If you could count the lineage of the all the descendants of Abraham, they would be as the sands of the sea and stars of heaven as God Promised to him. Just this fulfilled promised alone should make believers of all the skeptics.

I'm guessing because of Satan's past interference; God is not leaving anything to natural surrounding and growth. He has chosen a man to watch over and to build this man's family into a great Nation. I'm sure he knew this makes Satan's task a bit harder to accomplish than what Satan dealt with before the flood in Noah's days. However, you want to slice it, God has chosen a man to start this work; but before God will entrust his overall plan to this man, he will test this person to see how he measures up to God's standard. Oh yes, God tests people to see if they can cut it. The choice of Abraham by God wasn't by accident; God knew from the first earth age which of his sons he could depend on and placing the spirit of one of his elects wasn't a big gamble; but it was a gamble because even the elect has freewill. And because they don't know the part, they played in stopping the rebellion or even about the rebellion; they could have been led astray by Satan. Very little was known about the first earth age until Jeremiah and Ezekiel and Isaiah told of it in their works. And Christ gave information concerning this time period along with Paul and Peter; but at the time of Abraham, almost nothing was revealed.

First thing God told Abram was to leave Haran and Abram left. He took his wife and Nephew, Lot, and the servants he had acquired and went to the land of Canaan. Naturally, the land belonged to the descendants of Noah thru Canaan and already had a multitude of different tribes living in the land. The first thing God did was to take Abram upon a high mountain and told him to look all around him and as far as he could see was to be his land. God was going to give it to him and his children as an inheritance forever. I'm sure that Satan had his hand over his mouth and was snickering behind it at God because he knew Abram was seventy-five years old and his wife Sarai was no spring chicken either.

For the next fifteen years Abram traveled up and down the land with his herds and family even so far as to enter Egypt. Abram became very rich with gold, silver, and cattle because of God's blessing. He became so rich and the cattle so plentiful until Lot's herdsmen and Abram's herdsmen came close to blows over water and grass rights. To settle the dispute, Abram told Lot to take his people and herds and chose whatever direction he wanted and Abraham would go in the opposite direction so as not to have conflict with one another. As it is written,

> And Lot lifted up his eyes, and beheld all the plain of Jordan, that it was well watered every where, before the Lord destroyed Sodom and Gomorrah, even as the garden of the Lord, like the land of Egypt, as thou comest unto Zoar. (Genesis 13:10)

Lot let the beauty of his eyes overshadow the knowledge of the Lord's blessing, and he chose what looked good to him and didn't worry about what God might have in store for him. He did it his way.

Abram listened to God and followed God's instructions and moved his herd to the area of Hebron and depended on God to take care of him. It was while Abram was in Hebron that word came to him of Lot and his goods being captured by Chedorlaomer and his cohorts after they had defeated the kings of Sodom and Gomorrah along with three other kings. Abram took three hundred and eighteen trusted men of his house and rescued

Lot and the others and their goods which had been taken by Chedorlaomer and his bunch.

It was after his return from the rescue of Lot that he met "Melchizedek" in person for the

first time. We are told Melchizedek was a priest of the "Most High God" and Abram was

blessed by this priest. I have often wondered why Melchizedek (translated=King of

Righteousness) was in this area and the purpose. It always seemed to me God was dealing

with Abraham apart from his office as Melchizedek, High Priest; unless, the kings who

attacked Sodom and Gomorrah and the other cities were under orders from God because

of all the evil practices going on in this area. Your thoughts could be different from mine.

It was during this time Abram got a vision from God and we get a glimpse of the

eternal purpose of God. In a vision God told Abram,

> Look now toward heaven, and tell the stars, if thou be able to number: and he said
> unto him, so shall thy seed be. (Genesis 15:5)

And the bible said Abram believed him and God counted it to him for

"righteousness". Nothing has changed with God's way of doing things or in his way of

dealing with his children. God knows the flesh is weak, but we can still obtain

"righteousness" the same as Abram. All we have to do is "trust and obey", just like the

old song tells us. We obey by repenting of our wrongs and trusting God to forgive us and

help us live a better life with him in charge.

God has chosen Abram and his descendants to be his Nation and through these people God will enter this world physically to be with his children. The rest of the Old Testament is a history lesson on how this Nation was built; the many failures of its people and the ultimate rejection of the Nation as a whole. In the book of Ezekiel, we learn God married the city of Jerusalem and took her to be his wife. This marriage of Jerusalem is actually symbolic of God marrying the nation of Israel. And we read,

> I have caused thee to multiply as the bud of the field, and thou have increased and waxen great, and thou art come to excellent ornaments: thy breasts are fashioned, and thine hair is grown, whereas thou were naked and bare. Now when I passed by thee, and looked upon thee, behold, thy time was the time of love; and I spread my skirt over thee, and covered thy nakedness: yea, I sware unto thee, and entered into a covenant with thee, saith the Lord God, and thou became mind. (Ezekiel 16:7-8)

The first part of this chapter gives some details of when and how God chose this people to be his. I know the writings have the city of Jerusalem as its object, but that's all symbolic. Read this whole chapter sixteen in the book of Ezekiel and you'll see the love God has for his children and the hurt in his heart when they go whoring after other things instead of loving him.

God didn't leave things this way for very long. Like most men or women will do when their spouses go astray and become promiscuous and refuse to change their ways, God divorced his wife, the Nation of Israel. Yes, God is a divorcee' as stated in Jeremiah and we read,

> The Lord said also unto me in the days of Josiah the king, have you seen that which backsliding Israel has done? She is gone up upon every high mountain and under every green tree, and there has played the harlot. And I said after she had done all these things, turn thou unto me. But she returned not, and her treacherous sister Judah saw it. And I saw, where for all the causes whereby backsliding Israel committed adultery, I had put her away, and given her a "bill of divorce"; yet her treacherous sister Judah feared not, but went and played the harlot also. (Jeremiah 3:6-8)

But wait; Christ did come thru this Nation, didn't he? Yes and no, when Christ was born the Nation of Israel had been conquered and its people shipped off into a foreign land. They never returned to the land God gave them to be theirs forever. What happened to the promises he made to Abraham? O yes, they were fulfilled; look around you. All the Arab nations came from the loins of Abraham. The modern Nation of Israel came from Abraham also, and the nations of Russia and all Europe, including the Caucasian people of North and South America. And then we have the Nation of Australia and the peoples of Caucasian descent in South Africa and Canada. (For a further study on the migrations of the Nation of Israel known historically as the 10 Lost Tribes of Israel read the book 'Judah's Sceptre and Joseph's Birthright' by J H Allen as published by Destiny Publishers) In other words, most of the white races today have their origin from the loins of Abraham.

In order to bring you up to speed, let's talk about the Nation of Israel for a little while. God created this nation from Abram. After Abram had successfully pleased God by obeying him, (Genesis 26:5) God changed his name to Abraham and gave him a son and the son was named Isaac and he produced twin sons; the name of the first born was

Esau and the second one was Jacob. Esau was a hunter and cared very little about anything except his own selfish desires. For the most part, Russia holds most of the prodigy of Esau.

Because of his selfish attitude and rejection of his Heavenly Father, God rejected him from the birthright of Abraham, and after testing Jacob for many years while he was under the servitude of his mother's brother, Laban, he was accepted after proving himself to God, and then God changed his name from Jacob to Israel. Jacob produced 12 sons and the offspring of these sons became the 12 tribes of Israel.

Because God needed time for this new Nation of very few people to multiply without being destroyed or kept at a minimum strength, God placed them in the land of Egypt under the protection of the Pharaoh. At this time in history, Egypt was the strongest nation around. The old kingdom or the lower kingdom of Egypt had been conquered by an Adamic race from the region of modern-day Persia through Noah's son Japhet; these peoples were called Hyksos and ruled Egypt during the time of Joseph tenure, and the beginning of the small Nation of Israel. Joseph was one of the youngest sons of Jacob and the family thought him to be dead; his father, Jacob, didn't know his own brothers had sold him to some slavers and that they had carried him to Egypt. There he pleased the Pharaoh and after demonstrating his ability to govern, Pharaoh made him second ruler in the kingdom. Joseph married one of the Hyksos Princess, the daughter of Pharaoh, and his people the Nation of Israel lived peaceably for several hundred years as they grew in size and numbers. Eventually, the original rulers of Egypt regained control and placed the Israelites into slavery. It was from this slavery God brought his people out of and into the land he gave to Abraham. Of course, at this time it was called the land of Canaan.

After God brought these tribes from Egypt under the leadership of Moses, they conquered the land of Canaan under various leaders selected by God. God in symbolism married this Nation and in effect took her to be his wife. God as husband to this Nation guarded her and protected her from all the surrounding enemies. As much as God blessed his people, it seemed they couldn't help but do the wrong thing. He gave his people a law to live by and ten of the most famous commandants ever issued. They are still in effect today and if you keep them, you'll have a bountiful life. But strange as it may seem to some people, these children of God repeatedly left the fellowship of the true God and went a whoring after heathen gods. Eventually God rejected this Nation as a whole and gave her a bill of divorcement. This divorce is recorded in Jeremiah of which we have discussed above.

Some of the rulers of Israel were good leaders and some were not so good. King David was probably the ruler most pleasing to God. Although David was a sinner like all peoples in the flesh, he confessed his sin to God and asked for forgiveness. This owning up to the sins committed pleased God and David was promised a descendant of his would always sit on the throne of David. Some erroneously think Christ fulfilled this promise God mad to David; but, Christ has yet to sit on a throne. He didn't while he was in the flesh and walked the earth and although promised, he has not as yet sat on David's throne ruling the Nation of Israel.

What became of this Nation of Israel on whom God poured out so many blessings? His Nation or bride became an adulteress by their idol worship, and lost God's blessing in that they disobey the laws God set before them. This bride of God worshipped the gods of the lands God captured for them, and in God's eyes became a whore in his sight and God recoiled in anger.

Because of internal disputes and high taxes, the ten northern tribes split from the Nation of Israel; but they kept the title to the Nation. The remaining two tribes became know as the Nation of Judah after their ancestor Judah, one of the sons of Jacob. God allowed this; perhaps thinking one of the two Nations would come back and follow his laws and he would watch over them again. But they didn't and after several hundred years, God sent the Assyrian Nation to war against his people and all of the ten northern tribes were eventually lead away into slavery. Hundreds of years later, when the Assyrian Empire became weak, these same tribes migrated thru the Caucasus Mountains and spread over Europe becoming known as Bulgars, Alans, Suebi, Goths, Frisians, Franks, Scythians, Huns, Vandals, Sarmatians, and Thracians. These are the most numerous tribes originating from the Caucasus Mountains vicinity. These tribes spread over Europe and Russia and for the most part are the "white" races of today. And no wonder, for God said,

> For, lo, I will command, and I will sift the house of Israel among all nations, like as corn is sifted in a sieve, yet shall not the least grain fall upon the earth. (Amos 9:9)

So you see, we have lost our identity and don't know who we are; but God still knows where each and every child of his is today. Most of the prophecies given in the bible are about the Nation of Israel. God is not talking about the JEWS! The Jews belong to the Nation of Judah even though modern day Jews have named their country Israel; they are not the Nation of Israel in God's eyes.

Let's look at the remaining nation left in the promise land; the Nation of Judah. Did this nation do any better than her sister Israel? And the answer to this question is NO! Keep in mind that God is always fair; and his promise and commitment to his servant David has to be honored. He has promised David to keep a descendant of his on the throne of Israel until the eternal King claims this throne and rules forever. (2 Samuel 7:16) How will he do this since he has already disowned or as the bible states; God divorced his bride or the Nation of Israel. (Jeremiah 3:8) O, yes, I'll say it again, God is a divorcee! So, what does he do with this Nation of Judah which he has left to work with to carry out his plan to bring himself into this physical world of flesh?

First, he sends Nebuchadnezzar to take Judah captive and lead into Babylon Jehoiachin and his best smiths and Princes and mighty men of valor and craftsmen. In essences, Nebuchadnezzar claimed the best talented people of the land for himself. This met God's approval, because he wanted the best talented saved so he could use them at a later date for his on purpose. Nebuchadnezzar left Zedekiah in charge of Jerusalem to be a vassal king unto himself. Zedekiah broke his oath to Nebuchadnezzar and rebelled and had to be put down; him and all of his sons. His sons were all beheaded before Zedekiah and then Zedekiah's eyes were put out and he was carried away as a slave to Babylon. There was never to be a king ruling over the house of Judah in their homeland again. Did this end God's promise to David; some claim Christ fulfilled this promise, but in their misunderstanding of God's word, have got this part wrong. Christ never sat on a throne; he never ruled anything on earth, yet. So, he was not God's answer to this promise to David. What they have failed to pickup on is the prophet Jeremiah's commission. The bible states he was to take a tender twig and God would plant it. Our information comes from a parable given to Ezekiel, and we read,

> Thus, saith the Lord God; I will also take of the highest branch of the high cedar, and will set it; I will crop off from the top of his young twigs a tender one, and will plant it upon a high mountain and eminent: (Ezekiel 17:22)

This twig was one of the daughters of Zedekiah left in Jeremiah's care after the sons of Zedekiah were slain and he was carried blinded into Babylon. These daughters being left in Jeremiah's care is not a big step since Jeremiah was Zedekiah's grandfather. The book of Jeremiah ends with them and Jeremiah in Egypt. The bible doesn't tell us what happened to these daughters, but history states a priest from Egypt arrived in Ireland with three royal women of Israel and wed one of these daughters to the King of Ireland which was a descendant of Judah thru his son Zarah. The other two according to circular history went to Scotland and to Sweden and married into the ruling line. The throne of David is still alive and occupied; today it is occupied by Queen Elizabeth.

Even through God rejected this Nation of Israel which he had chosen to show the world the right way to live; he didn't reject Abraham's bloodline to be used to bring him into this physical world.

Part Three

The First Advent:

We have the Nation of Israel scattered to the four winds and the Nation of Judah in captivity to the Babylonians. I guess Satan is laughing his behind off at God and at God's children; and I'm sure he thinks he has nothing to worry about now. Well we'll see, won't we? Satan truly doesn't understand the power of God, does he?

Our Lord God spoke through his servant Isaiah 137 years before the event took place about his servant Cyrus whom he would raise up to do his bidding. God named him in his word and wrote down how he was to accomplish the deed God had in store for him. God speaking through Isaiah,

> Thus saith the Lord to his anointed, to Cyrus, whose right hand I have held, to subdue nations before him; and I will loose the loins of kings, to open before him the two leaved gates; and the gates shall not be shut; I will go before thee, and make the crooked places straight: I will break in pieces the gates of brass, and cut in sunder the bars of iron: and I will give thee the treasures of darkness, and hidden riches of secret places, that thou may know that I, the Lord, which call thee by thy name, am the God of Israel. For Jacob my servant's sake, and Israel mine elect, I have surnamed thee, though thou hast not known me. (Isaiah 45:1-4)

Circular history tells us when Cyrus attacked Babylon, he diverted the Tigress River into the Euphrates pushed open the two gates placed across the Tigress River to the top of the water and walked into Babylon with his whole army. Babylon was defeated in hours.

How is that for fulfilling a prophecy given one hundred and thirty-seven years before the event took place.

Seventy years after they are conquered, the Jews are released and told they can go back home and rebuild their temple. This they did under the leadership or Nehemiah and Ezra; but they were still under the rule of the Medes and Chaldeans. After the Medes and Chaldeans' rule came others who ruled them, and then the Greeks and finally the Romans were their Masters. They never had a king or were able to accomplish self rule until 1948 when they formed the modern Nation of Israel. For about twenty-six hundred years they had been cast out of their homeland and were governed by some other nation. What caused this calamity on the Jews?

It all began about 6 BC when a virgin girl became pregnant with a child conceived by the Holy Spirit; that is, God in the form of Spirit. They should have been ready; God's prophets had written of the coming event and given this prophecy to them hundreds of years before. But they weren't, they were like most of us; they couldn't see the forest for the trees.

Shepherds were told of the event and wise men from the east traveled around two years to give homage to the new King. Even Herod, the pulpit king placed in charge by the Romans believed the report of the wise men. He told the wise men to find the child and report back to him so he could come and worship the new King. The wise men were warned by God in a dream the true purpose of Herod and they took a different route back to their land.

Upon finding the baby Jesus, they presented him with gifts of gold, frankincense, and myrrh. An angel told Joseph in a dream that Herod was seeking the child to kill it and for Joseph to go to Egypt until he was told to come back. Do you think God doesn't provide for needs? The gold and other gifts left by the wise men were just what Joseph needed for travel expenses to Egypt and back.

The child's name was Jesus and everywhere he went crowds flocked to his side for healing and to listen to his word. As it reads,

...never man spake like this man?" (John 7:46)

He gave us the "Sermon on the Mount" and parables so we could learn how to live peacefully with our fellow man. He showed us the true meaning of God's written word. He didn't condemn sinners, but showed the sinner how to overcome and come out of sin. He raised people from the dead and told us he had conquered death. He told us about the Kenites and the way they work in our lives.

Whoa! Hold up a minute! Who are the Kenites? I don't believe I've heard of them before. You need to explain yourself. Well, I did mention them earlier, and yes you're right, I need to explain fully about who and what the Kenites are all about, but where to begin.

In a nutshell, the Kenites are the descendants of Satan through his son Cain and produced by Eve and a twin to Abel. (Strong Concordance # 7014 & 7017) They made it thru the flood of Noah's day (Genesis 15:19) and are mentioned again in the book of Joshua. In this book they use the family name of Gibeon instead of the National name of Kenites. I'll show you the connection as we move along. As Joshua led God's people out from the wilderness and into the promise land, he had to "take" the land from others who had already settled there. And as it reads,

> When the inhabitants of Gibeon heard what Joshua had done unto Jericho and to Ai, They did work wilily, and went and made as if they had been ambassadors, and took old sacks upon their asses, and wine bottles, old and rent, and bound up; and old shoes and clouted upon their feet, and old garments upon them; and all the bread of their provision was dry and moldy. And they went to Joshua unto the camp at Gilgal, and said unto him, and to the men of Israel, we be come from a far country: now therefore make a league with us. (Joshua 9:3-16)

These Kenites tricked Joshua into thinking they had come from a far away place, when in actuality they were close at hand and part of the bunch God had told Joshua to wipe out completely. Since they "hoodwinked" Joshua and the Princes of Israel into making a deal to spare them, Joshua had to honor their bargain and as it reads,

> And Joshua made peace with them, and made a league with them, to let them live: and the Princes of the congregation sware unto them. (Joshua 9:15)

So, since they couldn't break the vow they had made before God, there was only one thing left for them to do; and that was to accept them as slaves, which they did. But look where they put them to work of all places. And as it reads,

> And Joshua made them that day hewers of wood and drawers of water for the congregation, and for the altar of the Lord, even unto this day, in the place which he should choose. (Joshua 9:27)

How about that! Joshua put them right into the worship service next to God's altar to service it. Satan's children are taking care of the needs of God's priest. What irony?

In the book of Judges, we read of a Kenite called Heber moving unto the plain of Zaanaim. But the wording is a bit misleading. At first reading, the sentence seems to tell us Heber was a Kenite; but this is not what the scripture conveys at all. Heber is called a Kenite because he had been living in the "land belonging to the Kenites". It's just like I'm called a South Carolinian because I live in South Carolina. My bloodline is English, but it doesn't change where I live or what I'm known as. We are told Heber was also from the children of Hobab which was the father-in-law of Moses. In other scripture we learn Moses' father-in-law was a Midianite means Moses father-in-law descended from his ancestor Midian, a son of Abraham. I wanted to bring this terminology to mind here so we can grasp some of the wording we will run across later on. It is best to really check out what the bible is really telling us.

Our next meeting with the Kenites occurs in 1 Samuel while Saul is leading God's people as their king. God has told Saul thru Samuel to destroy all the Amalekites including all livestock, women, and children. Again, we read,

> And Saul said unto the Kenites, Go, depart, get you down from among the Amalekites, lest I destroy you with them: for ye showed kindness to all the children of Israel, when they came up out of Egypt. So the Kenites departed from among the Amalekites. (1 Samuel 15:6)

This event Saul has remembered is not found in the bible except we consider their meeting with Joshua to be the time to which Saul is referring. Any way you want to slice it, the Kenites escaped again. Remember God didn't tell Saul to let the Kenites go this time or in Joshua's case, to let them go at that time either.

We next run across these Kenites or maybe better said their descendants in the book of 1 Chronicles and here we see some more of their family names. As it is recorded in the bible,

> And the families of the scribes which dwelt at Jabez, the Tirathites, the Shimeathites, and Suchathites. These are the Kenites that came of Hemath, the father of the house of Rechab. (1 Chron. 2:55)

Besides the bible giving us more of the family names of the different tribes of Kenites, we find out they have been promoted from "wood hewer" and "water bearers" for the temple to scribes. The scribes had the task of keeping a record of all that happens to a nation; now you might have an idea why parts of the bible are hard to understand or seems misleading. Satan's hand is always at work.

We don't hear of these peoples being called Kenites any more in the bible. Why? Because they have changed their names and are now called something different. We find them being referred to as "nethinims" later on in 1 Chronicles. The word "nethinim" is from the Hebrew and translates to "given to service" in English language dictionary. The Kenites have lost their national identity and are still servants in the temple under the heading of "Nethinims". As we read, "Now the first inhabitants that dwelt in their possessions in their cities were the Israelites, the priests, the Levites, and the Nethinims." (1 Chronicles 9:2) Whoa! Why have the Nethinims cities; God never said anything about the children of Cain having cities of their own in among the Israelites. It didn't take Satan long to mix his brood in with God's children, did it?

We don't hear anymore about the "nethinims" as they are now called until we learn the children of Judah are going back to Jerusalem to rebuild the Temple of God. As it is written,

> Now in the first year of Cyrus, king of Persia, that the word of the Lord by the mouth of Jeremiah might be fulfilled, the Lord stirred up the spirit of Cyrus king of Persia, that he made a proclamation throughout all his kingdom, and put it in writing, saying thus saith Cyrus king of Persia, the Lord God of heaven hath given me all the kingdoms of the earth; and he hath charged me to build him an house at Jerusalem, which is in Judah. (Ezra 1:1-2)

When Ezra and his group lined up to return unto the promise land, he gave a list of the chief rulers of each clan with their genealogies intact and also a list of those who couldn't show they were blood descendants of Israel. You notice the Nethinims were among the ones who had good genealogies for their people. How! You forget who the scribes were, didn't you? Let me remind you again; they were the Kenites! Now, they call themselves, Nethinims!

Anyway, Ezra took his bunch of people out from captivity in Babylon and headed toward Jerusalem. This bunch numbered forty-two thousand three hundred and sixty persons. When they reached their destination, they began to build the House of God; but were halted by the peoples the Assyrian had placed there and the descendants left behind by Nebuchadnezzar when he first deported the tribe of Judah or Jews as they are now called. These people were considered mixed blooded and the Jews would have nothing to do with them. Later on, these people were called Samaritans because their capital was still located at Samaria. After the Temple was about finished, Ezra went back to Babylon to plead his case before Artaxerx the king, and winning approval came back to dedicate the Temple and to bring with him Chief men of Israel. This time Ezra stopped at the river (probably the Euphrates) and checked out who he had with him. Ezra found that he was going to dedicate the Temple without a Levitical priest. And so he sent back a Nethinim to the chief priest Iddo for ministers to the house of God. What he received was 38 sons of Levi and 220 more Nethinims.

Are you following what Satan is doing? We have 38 priests who are descended from Aaron and 220 "so called" workers or priests in God's House. It's no wonder God didn't bless this group very much; only enough to ensure his arrival in the flesh would be unhindered.

Are you still wondering about the Nethinims? Let's let the bible show us so there won't be any misunderstanding, and we see,

> Also, of the Nethinims, whom David and the princes had appointed for the service of the Levites, two hundred and twenty Nethinims: all of them were expressed by name. (Ezra 8:20)

We last hear of them living in Opel in the Old Testament.

Are we through with Cain's children? Have they faded off into the sunset of history; never to cause trouble again? Of course not, Satan thinks he has interfered in God's plan so much until he doesn't have to worry about the Father coming into this world as Savior. We all know the story of Christ's birth and how Satan tried to use Herod to kill him while he was still an infant and helpless. But God saw to it that this didn't happen. Later, when Jesus became a grown man and started his mission from God to be the sacrifice God would use to atone for the sins of his children, Satan tried to tempt him in the wilderness by asking Jesus to join his team and have all the world's riches. The physical Christ refused because he trusted his spiritual Father, who was residing inside of him, in all things. After being tempted by the Devil, Christ returned to Galilee and then to Nazareth. An in the synagogue there Christ proclaimed his mission and the start of his Kingdom. We read,

> The Spirit of the Lord is upon me, because he hath anointed me to preach the gospel to the poor; he hath sent me to heal the brokenhearted, to preach deliverance to the captives, and recovering of sight to the blind, to set at liberty those that are bruised, to preach the acceptable year of the Lord. (Luke 4:18 & 19)

Christ was quoting from Isaiah 61:1 & 2; but he didn't finish the last part of verse 2. Why? He didn't quote this part because this was not to take place yet. The last part would only happen if the people received Christ as Lord at this time. Do you know what the last part of verse 2 reads? Look it up; it's very interesting.

After causing a great disturbance in Nazareth to the extent the people of this town wanted to kill him for his claim; he traveled to Capernaum, a city of Galilee, saying,

> I must preach the kingdom of God to other cities also; for therefore am I sent. (Luke 4:43)

It wasn't long before the Temple priest had spies following Jesus around and asking questions in an effort to trip him up in his words; but Jesus could read their minds and never let them trap him. He always turned the tables on them and they fell in the trap.

Jesus traveled up and down the country of Palestine teaching and preaching the Kingdom of God. He preached this Kingdom was here already and for all people to believe and repent of their sins and to be baptized into the Kingdom. He had thousands of followers and they watched him do miracle after miracle, but few accepted his claim or joined his kingdom. Eventually, he met up with Satan's bunch in the Temple as he was teaching the people. The story is given in the book of John in chapter 8. The scriptures are a little confusing because Jesus is addressing two different groups and the way the

translation is done gives the impression its one group. We'll pick up the conversation

between Christ and the second group who as we'll see are not unknown to Christ. Christ

has just made the statement,

And ye shall know the truth, and the truth shall make you free. (John 8:32)

And they answer him, "We be Abraham's seed, and were never in bondage to any man: how sayest thou, ye shall be made free? (John 8:33)

Jesus answered them, verily, verily, I say unto you; whosoever committeth sin is the servant of sin. And the servant abideth not in the house forever: but the son abideth ever. If the Son therefore shall make you free, ye shall be free indeed. I know that ye are Abraham's seed; but ye seek to kill me, because my word hath no place in you. (John 8:34-37)

The confusing part of the scriptures which are a little vague is Christ saying the first

group he was teaching was descendants of Abraham and the second bunch only claimed

to be Abraham's descendants. Continuing on, Christ says,

I speak that which I have seen with my Father: and ye do that which ye have seen with your father. (John 8:38)

They answered and said unto him, Abraham is our father. (John 8:39)

Jesus saith unto them, if ye were Abraham's children, ye would do the works of Abraham. But now ye seek to kill me, a man that hath told you the truth, which I heard of God: this did not Abraham. Ye do the deeds of your father. (John 8:39-41)

Then said they to him, we be not born of fornication; we have one Father, even God. (John 8:41)

> Jesus said unto them, if God were your Father, ye would love me: for I proceeded forth and came from God; neither came I of myself, but he sent me. Why do ye not understand my speech? Is it even because ye cannot hear my word? Ye are of your father the devil, and the lusts of your father ye will do. He was a murderer from the beginning, and abode not in the truth, because there is no truth in him. When he speaketh a lie, he speaketh of his own: for he is a liar, and the father of it. And because I tell you the truth, ye believe me not. Which of you convinceth me of sin? And if I say the truth, why do ye not believe me? He that is of God heareth God's words: ye therefore hear them not, because ye are not of God. (John 8:42-47)

Jesus said their father was a murderer from the beginning; who was the first murderer? The answer is simple; it was Cain when he murdered Abel. So you see we still have the Kenites with us; only now they are calling themselves Jews and claiming to be descendants of Abraham. Jesus called them liars. Do you need a second witness from the bible? Ok; turn with me to the 1 epistle of John in chapter 3, and we read,

> Not as Cain, who was of that wicked one, and slew his brother, and wherefore slew he him? Because his own works were evil, and his brother's righteous. (1 John 3:12)

We all know who the "wicked one" is, don't we; it is none other then Satan or as some call him, the Devil. They were there in Jesus' days and they are still with us even today. Christ told us we would know them by their "fruits"; meaning by what they do.

Christ explained the mystery of the Kenites and their final end in his parable of the "Tares" and we'll look at this parable now. First, Christ gave this parable to a crowd of listeners which were gathered to hear him preach. This is the parable:

> The kingdom of heaven is likened unto a man who sowed good seed in his field: but while he slept, his enemy came and sowed tares among the wheat, and went his way. But when the blade was sprung up, and brought forth fruit, then appeared the tares also. So, the servants of the householder came and said unto him: Sir, didst not thou sow good seed in thy field? From whence then hath it tares? He said unto them, an enemy hath done this. The servants said unto him, wilt thou then that we go and gather them up? But he said, nay; lest while ye gather up the tares ye also root up also the wheat with them. Let both grow together until the harvest: and in the time of harvest I will say to the reaper, gather ye together first the tares and burn them: but gather the wheat into my barn. (Matthew 13:24-30)

It is noteworthy to add that this word "seed" is from the Greek word "sperma" and means the male sperm. "Sperma" is used so the average reader will understand Christ is separating two groups of people and he's not discussing wheat or any crop growing from the natural ground.

After the crowd Christ was teaching left the area, the disciples followed him into a house and inquired of him to explain the parable of the tares. Remember, when Christ explains something, there's no reason for farther discussion or trying to say; "this is what he really meant". The parable as Christ explained it:

> He that sowed the good seed is the son of man; the field is the world; the good seed are the children of the kingdom; but the tares are the children of the wicked one; the enemy that sowed them is the devil; the harvest is the end of the world; and the reapers are the angels. As therefore the tares are gathered and burned in the fire; so shall it be in the end of this world. The son of man shall send forth his angels, and they shall gather out of his kingdom all things that offend, and them which do iniquity; and he shall cast them into a furnace of fire: there shall be wailing and gnashing of teeth. Then shall the righteous shine forth as the sun in the kingdom of their Father. Who hath ears to hear, let him hear? (Matt.13:37-43)

A follow up is in Revelation where it reads,

> And I looked, and behold a white cloud, and upon the cloud one sat like unto the
> Son of man, having on his head a golden crown, and in his hand a sharp sickle.
> And another angel came out of the temple, crying with a loud voice to him that sat
> on the cloud, thrust in thy sickle, and reap: for the time is come for thee to reap;
> for the harvest of the earth is ripe. And he that sat on the cloud thrust in his sickle
> on the earth; and the earth was reaped. (Rev. 14:14-16)

Need I say more about the Kenites? Maybe just one other thought. In the book of

Revelation, we are shown seven Christian churches and Christ is only pleased with two

of these churches. I ask, what was so special about these two churches for Christ to be

pleased with them? The only thing these two churches had in common was what they

preached; could this make Christ happy? Maybe; so let's see what these two churches,

Smyrna and Philadelphia, were preaching,

> I know thy works, and tribulation, and poverty, (but thou are rich) and I know the
> blasphemy of them which say they are Jews, and are not, but are the synagogue of
> Satan. (Rev. 2:9)

It seems these two churches knew about the Kenites and were warning their people

to be on guard and this pleased Christ. Does your church teach about Satan's Children?

It states in the book of Job, "But there is a spirit in man: and the inspiration of the

Almighty giveth them understanding". And from the bible, we also know a human body

can house more then one spirit and this second spirit invades the flesh body by force. As

we read,

> And in the synagogue, there was a man, which had a spirit of an unclean devil,
and> cried out with a loud voice, saying, let us alone; what have we to do with thee,

thou Jesus of Nazareth? Art thou come to destroy us? I know thee who thou are; the Holy One of God. (Luke 4:33-34)

And in other places we are shown the same thing. One of the jobs Christ came to do was to gather spirits who had fled into this earth age and to ordered them back to a Heavenly prison to be held unto judgment day. Our reference for this thought is in the book of Jude and it reads,

And the angels who kept not their first estate, but left their own habitation, he hath reserved in everlasting chains under darkness unto the judgment of the great day. (Jude 1:6)

Ok, here's something just off the cuff; we know from scripture God places a spirit of one of his children from the first earth age into a newborn baby at conception and all humans contain a spirit inside their flesh body. We are not told who or the type of spirit God places inside a human baby; but, suppose God decided to use the physical offspring of Satan from the loins of Cain to house those angels who joined with Satan in the rebellion of the first earth age. Of Course, as I stated earlier, there is no biblical proof of this documented in God's word, but it would make more sense as to why certain individuals have acted the way they have in the past. This is just my thoughts; take them or leave them.

Jesus explained the concept of a spirit being placed into a new born baby at conception in his dialogue with Nicodemus. He explained all souls have to come from heaven and be born through woman by natural childbirth. The scriptures say "born again", but this is a mistranslation. The correct translation is "born from above". (Greek word "anothen") The Greek word actually infers to be from the very beginning; which, in out subject would be all the way back to the first earth age. God puts a spirit of one of his children he changed into spirit form at the end of the first earth age into each new born baby to see how they will fare in this physical age or second earth age. (Psalms 104:4) He explains to Nicodemus that nobody would enter into the Kingdom of God unless they were born of water and of the spirit. "Born of water" means the woman's water has to break in childbirth before the baby can come forth and enter this flesh world. Then at the death of this flesh body, the released spirit can go back to heaven. Jesus confirms his teaching by saying,

> And no man hath ascended up to heaven, but he that came down from heaven, even the Son of man which is in heaven. (John 3:3-13)

Christ is stating that the rules were not changed for him either; he had to come into this flesh age by being birthed in natural childbirth.

God in the human form of Jesus walked this earth for about thirty-three years. Three of those years he spent preaching and teaching the Kingdom of God was at hand. He healed the sick and raised the dead. Jesus showed the right way to live on this planet and he was rejected by almost all he talked to. The crowds followed him every where he went, but only for the food and healing he could provide. He became quite popular and because the religious leaders feared the loss of position and wealth, they plotted ways to get rid of him. As it is told, "He came unto his own, and his own received him not". (John 1:11) Finally, using a bribe to one of his close disciples, Judas, they were able to grab him without the crowds knowing about it. A hurried-up trial at night and persuading the Roman Procurator to give the death sentence, left the religious leaders of the Jewish Temple feeling they had won a great victory. The victory was not theirs; they had rejected the King and his Kingdom. They possibly had earned the reward of eternal death from the Father.

The following morning on the High Sabbath of Passover, the rejection became final as they witnessed the Roman execution of the Physical Son of God. The Kingdom on earth would not be established at this time.

The Kingdom Re-proclaimed:

I suspect the Religious leaders in Jerusalem felt pretty smug along about this time. The "thorn in their side" had been destroyed and no threat was visible on the immediate horizon of Temple life. There was some concern over the missing body of Jesus which had been reported to them, but they announced the condemned man's followers stole the body or at least they were going to stick to that story. Life was good, or so they thought, until they heard of a man fifty days later speaking to a crowd of people in the streets of Jerusalem. It was reported to them that even the foreigners from different lands heard this message in their own tongue. Lies! It was probably just lies being spread around. Still, there had been one by the name of Peter who claimed this so-called Jesus was alive. Peter claimed Jesus had been raised from the dead, and that he had walked and talk and even eaten dinner with him. Could these stories about Jesus being resurrected be possible?

I'm sure Satan quit rejoicing along about this time, because now, the one he thought was finished had been raised from the dead. The power of the one he was battling against was a lot stronger then he had imagined and now the charge of murder would be added to his list of crimes.

Later, we come across Peter and John going into the Temple and after being used by

the Holy Spirit to heal a man, Peter seizes the upon the opportunity to preach Jesus to a

large crowd which had gathered because of the miracle of healing. As it reads,

> When Peter saw it, he answered unto the people, ye men of Israel, why marvel ye at this? Or why look so earnestly on us, as though by our own power or holiness we had made this man to walk? The God of Abraham, and of Isaac, and of Jacob, the God of our fathers, hath glorified his Son Jesus; whom ye delivered up, and denied him in the presence of Pilate, when he was determined to   let him go. (Acts 3:12:13)

Peter, boldly, proclaims the Kingdom of God is at hand and everyone who repents of

their wrongs and believes on the name of Jesus will be saved. We find these same

teachings a major theme in the book of Acts,

> Repent ye therefore, and be converted, that your sins may be blotted out, when the times of refreshing shall come from the presence of the Lord; and he shall send Jesus Christ, which before was preached unto you: Whom the heaven must receive until the times of restitution of all things, which God hath spoken by the mouth of all his holy prophets since the world began. (Acts 3:19-21)

Repent is a word often used, but few people really understand the true meaning of

the word. Literally, it means to change direction, and to go about things in reverse order.

In discussing sin, it means to loathe the sin so much, to even think of what has taken

place is enough to make you sick to your stomach. It's a strong embarrassment to you

because Jesus knows what you have done and you hate to see him look upon you. But if

you have repented, and if you have asked for forgiveness, Jesus will look on you with

love in his eyes and say "yes, come on in, I have plenty of room for you with me".

The religious leaders of the Temple found to their amazement that the killing of Jesus didn't stop the proclaiming of the Kingdom of God to be established on earth. Jesus' disciples were preaching the same message Jesus preached and healing the sick as Jesus had done. In their eyes, nothing had changed but the death of Jesus, and now his disciples were claiming he had risen from the dead. Their whole plan had backfired.

Later on Peter and John were again preaching in the temple and healing all manner of sickness and casting out evil spirits until the crowds were so large the attention of the high priest and the Sadducees begin to take notice of the huge crowds and the disciple's popularity. This caused the high priest to have them arrested again and placed into prison. While in prison the Angel of the Lord came and released them. He told them,

> Go, stand and speak in the temple to the people all the words of this life". (Acts 5:20)

The disciples did as they were instructed and entered the temple early in the morning and began to teach the gospel of Christ because he is this life. Later the same morning, the high priest came and called the council together and sent for Peter and John. But they were not there in the prison and the high priest was told the men they sought were in the temple preaching Jesus Christ. Peter and John were arrested again by the temple guards, but without violence because they feared the people would rescue the disciples and stone the soldiers.

In answer to the charges against them about preaching Jesus, Peter and John answered, saying,

> We ought to obey God rather then men. The God of our fathers raised up Jesus, whom ye slew and hanged on a tree. Him hath God exalted with his right hand to be Prince and a saviour, for to give repentance to Israel and forgiveness of sins. And we are his witnesses of these things; and so is also the Holy Spirit, whom God hath given to them that obey him". (Acts 5:29-32)

I might point out here that the above verse stated "repentance to Israel"; this is not necessarily talking about the Jews. It may be a little confusing, but there are 12 tribes in Israel and all Jews are part of Israel but only one-twelfth of Israel is made up on Jews. Most of places in the bible which are referring to Jacob mean the whole Nation of Israel. All 12 tribes are included and when only Judah is mentioned, it means only the tribe of Judah and the tribe of Benjamin is involved. The bible usually refers to Ephraim if only the ten northern tribes are of concern. The ten northern tribes kept the name Israel. Most bible "thumpers" teach the bible is referring to the Jews all the way through the scriptures when in fact most of the time God is referring to the other branch, that is, the ten northern tribes. Don't forget, God doesn't lose anything; he knows where all his children are located.

Now, you can imagine how the priests felt when they heard the words of Peter. It cut them to their hearts and they took council to slay the disciples. Nice church folks, huh? Yeah, I know; more people have been killed over religion then in wars or for other reasons. But one Pharisee, Gamaliel, whom Paul had studied under, reasoned with them to do nothing. Because, Gamaliel stated, if this teaching was from God it couldn't be stopped, and if it was of man it would dissipate on its own. So Peter and John were beaten and turned loose. (Acts 5:34-40) But these beatings didn't the disciples, they taught daily in the temple and in every house, they ceased not to teach and preach Jesus Christ. (Acts 5:42)

The Kingdom of God was being proclaimed daily and God was adding to the church a great many disciples in Jerusalem. And also it states, a great company of the priests were obedient to the faith. It was during this time Stephen came into conflict with so-called Jews from the Synagogues of Libertines, and Cyrenians, and Alexandrians, and Cilicia and Asia. They are called Jews because of several possibilities. They could have been born in the land of Judah, or had accepted the Jewish faith; they were not necessarily of the bloodline of Judah. These men were unable to contradict Stephen's teachings, so they hired men to lie about what Stephen taught and had him delivered up to the council. Then they brought forth false witnesses and had him convicted on a charge of blasphemy. When Stephen answered the charge against him, he gave a very impressive sermon to the council. He ended his defense by saying,

> Ye stiff-necked and uncircumcised in hearts and ears, ye do always resist the Holy Spirit: as your fathers did, so do ye. Which of the prophets have not your fathers persecuted? And they have slain them which shewed before of the coming of the Just One; of whom ye have been now the betrayers and murderers: who have received the law by the disposition of angels, and have not kept it". (Acts 7:51-53)

These words cut the so-called Jews to the quick and they ran onto Stephen in a rage, gnashing him with their teeth and carried him out and stoned him to death. Saul, later called Paul and a student of Gamaliel, was one of the ones consenting to his death.

We all know of Saul's conversion on the road to Damascus (Acts 9:1-6) and the great preacher he became for Christianity. What I want to show or remind you of is Paul's mission from Christ; that is, what God told Ananias when he sent Ananias to put his hand on Saul in order for Saul to receive his sight. In a vision, the Lord said to Ananias,

> Arise, and go into the street which is called Straight, and enquire in the house of Judas for one called Saul, of Tarsus: for, behold, he prayeth, and hath seen in a vision a man named Ananias coming in, and putting his hand on him, that he might receive his sight. (Acts 9:11-12)

Ananias knew who Saul was and told the Lord how much evil Saul had done,

> But the Lord said unto him, go thy way: for he is a chosen vessel unto me, to bear my name before the Gentiles, and kings, and the children of Israel: for I must shew him how great things he must suffer for my name's sake". (Acts 9:15-16)

Notice, Saul (Paul) has a three-fold mission and the last of his orders were to witness before the "children of Israel". Again, I remind you the "Jews" are not the house of Israel but are only a small portion of it. In the book of Acts, we have Paul witnessing before Kings and Gentiles and a few of the Jews, most of these were Kenites disguised as Jews and claimed to be Jews as they did when Christ spoke to them. What about the "children of Israel"? Did Paul complete his mission from Christ? The book of "Acts" stops at the end of chapter 28 without the usual salutations. Historically, we find evidence of Paul being in the islands of Great Britain. There are ancient churches, St. Paul's Cathedral for one, with his name and legends of Paul preaching to the Druids on Mount Lud. In the Scottish declaration of Independence, the Scotts refer to themselves as being "of Israel" and date their history from the Exodus, but in it the term used is "the outgoing of the people of Israel". In this document, the Scotts also consider their country to be the "utmost part of the world". Was this Island of Brits and Scotts the "utmost part of the world" Christ spoke of in giving Paul his commission? We'll probable never know for sure, but we do know from historical records Christianity was wide spread in the British Isles.

In the year AD 42, Claudius, Emperor of the Romans, issued his fateful decree that the acceptance of the Druidic or Christian faith was a capital offense, punishable by death. Christians were to be killed by the sword, the torture chamber, or to be thrown to the lions in the arena of the coliseum. In his edict, Claudius ordered the complete destruction of Christian Britain. (The Lost Chapter of Acts by E. Raymond Capt)

The gospel spread into Africa and as it is written;

> And the angel of the Lord spake unto Philip, saying, arise, and go toward the south unto the way that goeth down from Jerusalem unto Gaza, which is desert. (Acts 8:26)

We know the story, the eunuch from Ethiopia was converted to Christianity and baptized and carried the word of Christ back with him to Ethiopia.

> But Philip was found at Azotus: and passing through he preached in all the cities, till he came to Caesarea." (Acts 8:40)

We have an example of God using a gentile named Cornelius of the Italian band to proclaim the good news in his direction among the Italians. History informs us the Italians were the peoples in Italy before the Romans moved in and took control. The bible tells us Cornelius was a devout man and one who feared (revered) God and his whole household was the same. We are told he saw a vision of an angel about the ninth hour (3:00 PM) and in the vision he was to send men to Peter at Joppa and Peter would tell him how to be saved. This he did and Peter came and preached Jesus Christ to them; and we read,

> To him give all the prophets' witness, that through his name whosoever believeth in him shall receive remission of sins. While Peter yet spake these words, the Holy Spirit fell on all them which heard the word. And they of the circumcision which believed were astonished, as many as came with Peter, because that on the Gentiles also was poured out the gift of the Holy Spirit. (Acts 10:43-45)

Christ's Kingdom began to spread throughout all the countryside as we see in this verse of the bible;

> Then had all the churches rest throughout all Judaea and Galilee and Samaria, and were edified; and walking in the fear (revere) of the Lord, and in the comfort of the Holy Spirit, were multiplied". (Acts 9:31)

So, we again see the Kingdom of God being re-proclaimed to the world even through the King has been killed and resurrected and has gone "into a far country". Remember the parable Christ gave about the vineyard being let out to husbandry and the king going on a far journey? This parable was about him.

For the readers who are not familiar with this parable of Christ, it reads,

> Hear another parable: there was a certain householder, which planted a vineyard, and hedged it round about, and digged a winepress in it, and built a tower, and let it out to husbandmen, and went into a far country: and when the time of the fruit drew near, he sent his servants to the husbandmen, that they might receive the fruits of it. And the husbandmen took his servants, and beat one, and killed another, and stoned another. Again, he sent other servants more then the first: and they did unto them likewise. But last of all he sent unto them his son, saying, they will reverence my son. But when the husbandmen saw the son, they said among themselves, this is the heir; come, let us kill him, and seize on his inheritance. And they caught him, and cast him out of the vineyard, and slew him. When the lord therefore of the vineyard cometh, what will he do unto those husbandmen? (Matthew 21:33-40)

The Kingdom again rejected and Israel again scattered:

Thus, the Kingdom having been re-proclaimed was again rejected by the religious community; but the gospel spread in other directions.

The rest of the book of Acts deals with Paul and other disciples teaching and preaching the gospel of Christ and through Satan's effort, the mainstream of the population rejected Jesus and Christianity. I can see no other reason for the violent attacks on Christianity except Satan was behind it.

Hardly had Paul been called by Christ into the ministry of spreading the gospel of Christ's kingdom, until the Jews took council to kill him. These Jews are most likely "Jews" by location only; most likely they are from the same bunch of the Kenites Christ described in John 8:44. And even though Saul was mistrusted by the Christian sect, they still helped him escape Damascus by lowering him over the wall of the city in a basket. (Acts 9:25)

On Paul's first missionary journey with Barnabas to Cyprus to preach the word of God in the synagogues of the Jews, they came upon a Jew whose name was Barjesus (Son of Jesus). He was with the deputy of the country, a man called Sergius Paulus who wanted to hear Paul preach the word of God. As it reads,

> But Elymas the sorcerer (for so is his name by interpretation) withstood them, seeking to turn away the deputy from the faith. Then Saul, (who is also called Paul) filled with the Holy Spirit, set his eyes on him, and said, O full of all subtly and all mischief, thou child of the devil, thou enemy of all righteousness, wilt thou not cease to pervert the right ways of the Lord". (Acts 13:9-10)

Paul called him what he was, a child of the devil; that is a Kenite.

Later Paul and Barnabas came to Antioch and preached Jesus in the local synagogue to the crowd. They taught Christ was the Son of God by showing the prophecies concerning him in the scriptures. Paul explained from the scriptures how the crucification and consequently the resurrection of Christ from the dead fulfilled the prophecies of Isaiah and other prophets. But Paul was not received in a good light by the Jews in the synagogue, but as we read in Acts 13,

> And when the Jews were gone out of the synagogue, the Gentiles besought that these words might be preached to them the next Sabbath. Now when the congregation was broken up, many of the Jews and religious proselytes (Gentiles who believed in God) followed Paul and Barnabas: who, speaking to them, persuaded them to continue in the grace of God. But when the Jews saw the multitudes, they were filled with envy and spake against those things which were spoken by Paul, contradicting and blaspheming. (Acts 13:42-45)

This envy and jealousy come from only one place; that is, from the tree of knowledge of good and evil. The Kingdom is again rejected by Jewish Israel. What was Paul and Barnabas reaction to the Jews at Antioch to their preaching the word of God?

Well, let's let Paul and Barnabas tell you in their own words,

> Then Paul and Barnabas waxed bold, and said, it was necessary that the word of God should first have been spoken to you: but seeing ye put it from you, and judge yourselves unworthy of everlasting life, lo, we turn to the Gentiles. (Acts 13:46)

And what do you think the Jews did about this rather rash statement? As it is written,

> But the Jews stirred up the devout and honorable women, and the chief men of the city, and raised persecution against Paul and Barnabas, and expelled them out of their coasts". (Acts 13:50)

Next, Paul and Barnabas traveled to Iconium and preached in the Jews synagogue and a great number of Jews and Greeks believed, but the unbelieving Jews stirred up the Gentiles, and made their minds evil affected against the brethren. It got so bad at Iconium; they had to flee to keep from being stoned. Next, they went to Lystra where they healed a cripple through the power of God. When the people saw the miracle, they believed Paul and Barnabas to be gods and would have done anything Paul asked of them. But there came certain Jews (Kenites) from Antioch and Iconium who persuaded the people not to believe the message of the Apostles and had them thrown out of the city and stoned, and left for dead.

It was probably at this time when Paul was thought "dead" that he had his vision of Heaven. This is the place where Paul writes that he knew a man in Christ fourteen years ago and he couldn't tell whether the man was in the spirit or in his physical body. Anyway Paul says the man was caught up to the third heaven and he heard unspeakable words which he couldn't retell. (2 Cor. 12:2)

I might add here there is only one heaven, but different heaven ages and for Paul to say he was in the third heaven, he had to be seeing a vision of heaven at the end of the Millennium or second earth age; there was a heaven in the first earth age and there is a heaven in this present earth age and there will be a heaven in the third earth age. God only created one heaven; (Genesis 1:1) but, there are different things happening in each earth age. This vision Paul saw of the third Heaven was not a vision of the future, but a vision of the future as God will make it. As I have said earlier in this writing, God is not a time traveler, but makes the future as he wants it to be.

Paul is carrying the word of God in every part of the country, but don't count Satan and his little workers out of the picture. As we are all human with flaws, Paul was also flawed in that he had been raised under the schooling of Gamaliel and like the rest of us; he was a bit hard-headed. He was warned by God twice not to go to Jerusalem, but Paul was determined to go and be there at the day of Pentecost. (Acts 21:4-11) Why would Paul want to keep Pentecost; this holiday was nothing to the Christian world Paul was helping set in place. To make matters worse, Paul agree to take the vows of a Nasserite; which was another custom which had no place in Christianity. As you would expect, Satan picked this time for his followers from Asia (Acts 21:27) to arrive in Jerusalem and when they saw Paul, they quickly began a loud protest and stirred up the people against Paul. These are the same Jews from Ephesus, Thyatira, Thessalonica, Iconium, and Antioch who had already tried to kill Paul once or twice before. Now that they had him in

Jerusalem, they were determined to kill him before he could leave the city and would have if God had not sent the Roman soldiers to his rescue. He was still going to Rome as God had instructed, but now he would go in chains. It was while Paul was in prison that he wrote most of the Pauline letters we still have today in the New Testament. I put this in because I wanted you to see God made use of a bad situation to do good for all concerned. We need to follow this example and work for the Kingdom wherever we find ourselves located.

This part of Paul's life was around 44 AD to 54 AD; we know because Claudius Caesar was ruling Rome at this time. And it would only be a few years until Nero would come into power and most of the Christian converts would be killed in the Roman coliseums for the pleasure of the disgruntled crowds. And then in 66 AD, a Roman general named Titus would attack Jerusalem because of the Jewish rebellion and at this time the Temple would be destroyed. It has never been rebuilt and the Jews were scattered all over the world and never returned to their homeland in great numbers until after WW II was over. Then in 1948, the present Nation of Israel was established and after about 2500 years, the Jews have a nation under their rule once more.

Why is it important that the Jews once again have their homeland under their control and are governing it by their own peoples? This date of the proclamation of the "new" Nation of Israel being established is one of the earmarks of the count down to the end of this second earth age. God told us through Jeremiah this reforming of the Jews or this

Nation of Judah would be a marker to the end or the start of the culmination of this physical age. As it is stated in Jeremiah,

> Thus saith the Lord, the God of Israel: like these good figs, so will I acknowledge them that are carried away captive of Judah, whom I have sent out of this place into the land of the Chaldeans for their good. For I will set mine eyes upon them for good, and I will bring them again to this land: and I will build them, and not pull them down; and I will plant them, and not pluck them up. (Jeremiah 24:5-6)

This happened in 1948 and Christ said this generation would still be alive when he returned to claim his kingdom. As Mark records Christ's word in his epistle, it states,

> Now learn a parable of the fig tree: when her branch is yet tender, and puts forth leaves, ye know that summer is near: so ye in like manner, when ye shall see these things come to pass, know that it is near, even at the doors. Verily I say unto you, that this generation shall not pass, till all these things be done". (Mark 13:28-30)

Peter, according to history was crucified upside down; James was beheaded; and the other disciples met a similar fate. John, one of the last survivors was locked up on Pathos Island and died there around 95 AD. It seemed Satan was winning battle after battle. And keep in mind Satan's main weapon is deceptions and half-truths. The things his people preach and teach sound so religious and good, but they are not the whole truths as set out in God's word. One of his best tools is in publishing "new bibles", so a word or two here should suffice; all bibles translated from the Hebrew and Greek can be changed a little here and a little there and the average reader will not notice the difference.

So, how do we tell if the bible we are studying is a correct translation or not? You can't unless you can go into the Hebrew and Greek to find out for yourself. Fortunately, the King James Bible has a concordance furnished by Dr. James Strong. In this

Concordance Dr. Strong has translated every word in the King James Bible back into the original languages for all to use. If you use the Strong's concordance as your reference text, you can decide yourself what is right in the King James Bible and what should have been translated differently. The King James Bible has a lot of errors in it but with the help of the Strong's concordance, you can get God original message to his children. None of the rest of the bibles on the market today has this kind of help for the average scholar to use. And, don't expect the 'New King James Bible" to be of any help; it has already been changed so much, Dr. Strong's work won't be of much help. Also, make sure you get an original Dr. Strong's concordance and not one of those 'new' or 'revised' Strong's concordances.

Christianity was spreading around the world, but not in the same character or freedoms Christ proclaimed. Legalism was being added and certain days to worship were being set. I doubt Paul, had he been around, would hardly have recognized the new faith by the second century AD. Sunday, the first day of the week, became the Christian Sabbath as proclaimed by the Bishop at Rome around 330 AD. The historical records claim this was done to separate the Christian religion from the Jewish religion as far as possible. At this same time of council meetings, the pagan feast of Ishtar was changed to Easter and the rites of Passover were done away with. 'Easter' being celebrated as the day Christ resurrected from the tomb. Anybody who takes the time to check out the different 'Sabbaths' of the Lord at the time Christ was crucified will easily see and under stand Christ was crucified on a Wednesday afternoon and resurrected late Saturday evening just before the sun dipped below the horizon. According to Jewish custom, the new day started just after the sun set.

The Kingdom Postponed and in Abeyance:

John was the last of the original disciples which were with Christ in the flesh. He has been imprisoned on the isle of Patmos, and it is there he receives his vision for the end times or the last message from Christ to his church. The message is given in the last book of the bible and it is the book we call Revelation. In this book of Revelation, we learn there are a lot of things which will have to happen on this earth before Christ is to return and claim his Kingdom.

The book of Revelation is written mostly in symbols, but, we are not left to interpret these symbols as we see fit. The meaning of each and every symbol is given somewhere in God's Holy Word. Our task is to find them and use them to get full knowledge of the message Christ left for his followers.

We are not going to do a study on Revelation in this setting, but we will mention or pull certain phrases from this material as needed to explain necessary text. Having stated this, let's move on in our study of God's eternal purpose.

Paul started his ministry preaching the immediate return of Christ to claim his Kingdom and it was probably about halfway thru his time of teaching before it was revealed to him that Christ was not returning to claim his church for a very long time, even hundreds, perhaps thousands of years.

We see Paul starting to address this return of Christ in the first book of Thessalonians where he is answering questions about where the dead are. It seems some of the brethren believed only the living could be part of the Kingdom and their loved ones who had died in the flesh were lost forever because Christ had not returned as yet. We read Paul's answer,

> I would not have you to be ignorant, brethren, concerning them which are asleep, that ye sorrow not, even as others, which have no hope. For if we believe that Jesus died and rose again, even so them also which sleep in Jesus will God bring with him. For this we say unto you by the word of the Lord that we which are alive and remain unto the coming of the Lord shall not prevent (precede) them which are asleep."(1 Thess. 4:14-15)

Who is God going to send back with Christ when he returns to earth? He will send all the ones who have died believing in the Christ as Lord and Savior. How can God do this; aren't the dead out somewhere in their graves waiting for the return of Christ? Of course not; as the bible states, instantly, when the body dies, the spirit returns to God who gave it. Our scripture is,

> ...because man goeth to his long home, and the mourners go about the streets: or ever the silver cord be loosed, or the golden bowl be broken, or the pitcher be broken at the fountain, or the wheel broken at the cistern. Then shall the dust return to the earth as it was: and the spirit shall return unto God who gave it. (Eccl. 12:5-7)

The first part of this scripture depicts symbolically different sayings for the death of a man, and the last part tells us in no short order that all spirits return to God at the death of the flesh. We that are alive can't precede the ones who have already died because they are already with Christ.

And again, Paul addresses this subject of Christ's return,

> Now we beseech you brethren, by the coming of our Lord Jesus Christ, and by our gathering together unto him. That ye be not soon shaken in mind, or be troubled, neither by spirit, nor by word, nor by letter as from us, as the day of Christ is at hand. Let no man deceive you by any means: for that day shall not come, except there come a falling away first, and that man of sin be revealed, the son of perdition; who opposeth and exalteth himself above all that is called God, or that is worshipped: so that he as God, shewing himself that he is God". (2 Thess. 2:1-4)

So you see the physical kingdom which is to be established on this very earth is in abeyance and has been postponed to some time in the future as this date has been set by God. Christ said He didn't know this date when he walked the earth in the flesh and that the angels didn't know, only the Father knew; but the seasons he would tell you, and the seasons of his return are mostly what the book of Revelation is all about. But we will cover some of it in this commentary.

From AD 100 to AD 300, there was a lot of turmoil in the Christian arena; some of the leaders of the churches Christ's disciples started have been executed and others are in hiding. Of the new comers, only Jerome has any influence and has the blessings of the early writers. The majority of the local Christian churches Paul established have been destroyed and its members have fled to the far reaches of the Roman Empire. We can only see Satan's hand in this persecution and destruction. New alliances were being made with one group claiming their teachings were correct and another group claiming theirs was the correct path to Heaven.

During the second century, the church struggled to survive as paganism once again surfaced throughout the Roman world. Satan used his wily efforts to destroy Christianity by gradually instituting devices similar to what Christ taught. As he tempted Christ in the wilderness with bible scriptures which were not quoted correctly, he urged the leaders of the Christian flock to insist on abeyance to their leaders. Ignatius, a bishop of the church at Antioch for forty years, was one of the most outspoken ones. He commanded all Christians everywhere to obey their bishops, the presbytery, and the deacons. These orders were straight out of Satan's book; Christ came to serve, not to be served. (Luke 12:37; Luke 22:25-27) Ignatius did well also; he opposed "Docetism", which claims Christ came as a spirit and not in the flesh. Another of Satan's tricks; go along with what everybody knows as truth and twist things not so certain. Ignatius was devoured in the Roman Coliseum by lions according to legend. After Ignatius, came other outspoken leaders of the Roman world who taught and preached their version of Christianity.

Some of the most noteworthy of this time period were Clement and Origen of Alexandria. Clement tried to harmonize the Greek paganism and Christianity by showing each could work together. He preached and taught that all religious beliefs were like streams flowing into a large river, and Christ was that river. Origen taught all would be saved eventually, even the Devil. He believed all things were independent of each other and were on a long homeward journey back to God, including the sun, moon, and all the stars of the universe. He did have an idea which carried over to the present. He is the first to "canonize" the writings of his day to which were the most important. His canon included all the present-day books of the New Testament as acceptable except Hebrews, James, 2 Peter, 2 John, 3 John, and Jude. Origen was labeled a heretic quite often and in the sixth century, Justinian the Byzantine emperor anathematized anyone who accepted Origen's doctrine.

The Roman Empire continued to expand during the first and second century AD and in doing so, brought in a variety of religions and beliefs. Most of these beliefs were accepted by Rome as long as these people acknowledged the Roman gods were superior to all other gods. There were only two sects which refused to accept the Roman gods. They were the Jews and the Christians. Many untruths were spread concerning both religions with the Christians being hit the hardest. Some say the Jews were an older religion and proved to be no threat to the Empire, while the Christians were a dangerous and subversive threat to all peoples, including the overthrow of the Empire.

We can see the hand of the Devil in sporadic persecutions all over the Roman Empire. Polycarp was martyred around 156 AD near present day Izmir, Turkey, nearly forty years after Ignatius died. Another was the martyrs of Lyons, Gaul (present day

France) where an untold number of Christians died for their faith. It is well noted the third century theologian Tertullian stated, "The blood of the martyrs is the seed of the church". Although Satan was having a "hey-day" by ensuring a large flow of Christian blood, these savage deaths attracted new converts and gave them the strength to endue.

Paganism also flourished and the mystery religions of Persia entered Rome. These mystery religions were not new but were a continuing presence of "sun" worshippers going all the way back to the days of Noah from the Old Testament. This ancient religion started with Nimrod, the great-grandson of Noah through his son Ham. The bible reads,

> And Cush begat Nimrod: he began to be a mighty one in the earth. He was a mighty hunter before the Lord: wherefore it is said, even as Nimrod the mighty hunter before the Lord. And the beginning of his kingdom was Babel, and Erech, and Accad, and Calneth, in the land of Shinar". (Genesis 10:8-10)

Nimrod was a builder of cities and formed the first world empire on earth. His physical strength undoubtably was very great and the people gathered to him for protection from animals and thieves of the day. Genesis 10:9 speaks of his reputation as a mighty hunter. Although, some scholars translate the word "hunter" as "adversary"; in that, Nimrod was a great adversary of our Lord. The evidence remains that Nimrod was a strong person in strength and will. It was Nimrod who contrived the idea of gathering the people into walled cities to protect them from the evils of the day, be it animals or murderers and thieves. Leaders of Freemasonry claim that this Nimrod was the founder of what is known today as the lodge of Freemasonry.

For we read in Albert Mackey's HISTORY OF FREEMASONRY, on page 601, "The Legend of the CRAFT in the Old Constitutions refers to NIMROD as one of the founders of Masonry."

As a great deliverer and protector of the people, this Nimrod became the first world dictator, with Babel or as we know it today, Babylon, being his main headquarters and Erech, Accad, Calneth the next cities of importance. This was in the land of Shinar or what is considered Iran and Iraq of the modern world. (Gen.10:8-11)

We all know power corrupts and absolute power corrupts absolutely. And so it was with Nimrod, His power was so great until he begin to consider himself a god and led his followers away from the true God of his great-grandfather Noah. (Josephus, Antiquities 1:4:2) He enlarged the system of study of the stars and astrology into occultism and hero worship. Only a few people living today understand God's plan for the salvation and reconciliation of his children has always been written in the stars for all to see. (Witness of the stars by E. W. Bullinger) The Tower of Babel was built under his supervision for the purpose of surviving another flood. He didn't want the people depending on some invisible God, but to depend on him as their Lord and Master. Nimrod would save them and receive their adoration and worship. Of course, we all know Satan was ruling Nimrod's mind and using him to discredit the true Lord.

Nimrod's plan caused God to come to earth and see first hand the mess Nimrod was making on earth. It is because of this we read in Genesis 11:4-9 that God scattered the people to form the various nations and confounded their language. As we will see, when God scattered the people, they took aspects of this Babylon Mystery Religion with them. We see later on in this discussion the details of the "Babylon Mystery" religion Nimrod and his wife, Semiramis, formed; and the start of the counterfeit Mother and child worship still in some churches today. Even outside of "so called" Christian churches, missionaries have been stunned to find this practice of the mother/child cult being carried forth in countries where no known missionaries have been teaching or working. (The Two Babylon's by Hislop)

OK, now let's get a bit more information on this mystery religion and why it's damaging to Christian lives and blocking their relationship with our Heavenly Father. So, what do we know about this Babylonian Religion Nimrod and his wife founded? Secular history and tradition tell us that Nimrod married a beautiful, blond-haired woman who was as evil and demonic as any who have ever walked this earth! Her name was Semiramis and under her guidance, Nimrod contrived a system whereby she, Nimrod, and her son would be objects of worship! Knowing God's promise of a future Savior (Gen.3:15), she claimed that Tammuz, her son, fulfilled this prophecy.

Babel, now called Babylon, was the center of Nimrod's kingdom and here in this city, Semiramis masterminded the forming of a religion based on God's promises, but twisted just enough to lead the people into worshipping them as "God" and the "Queen of Heaven". Their son, Tammuz, would fulfill the role of the savior of the world, or he would be the promised "Messiah" of Genesis 3:15. This is all spelled out in detail in a well-documented book entitled 'THE TWO BABYLONS by Alexander Hislop. It can be purchased from CHICK PUBLICATIONS at www.chick.com., and also, by calling 909-987-0771. It documents how she, Semiramis, developed a system of a celibate Priesthood which was answerable to her and the High Priest, Nimrod, who was known by the title of 'Pontiff' or Pontifex Maximus, meaning "bridge-maker". This High Priest Nimrod was supposedly the 'BRIDGE' between this life and the life to come. He was also known as the fish god, "DAGON"; this is why a fish-mitre hat was worn by the High Priest. We still see these fish-mitre hats worn by priests today! It was in the shape of a fish's open mouth. Semiramis knew an unmarried celibate priesthood would be more devoted to the religion and to her and her husband. Hislop tells us the regular priests wore black robes, which was the color of Satanism & the occult. (Fausset's Bible Ency.p291). Hislop also documents that Nimrod had a council of twelve priests to assist him in the temporal and political affairs of running the empire, and they were called "CARDINALS' and they were dressed in scarlet & red robes (Hislop, p210).

Another distinguishing mark of the priests of Nimrod, later known in the Old Testament as Priests of Baal, was the Clerical tonsure, an initiation rite in which the priest of Nimrod has the top of his head sheared bald, while the edges of the hair allowed to remain as a ring...in honor to Nimrod who was also worshipped as the SUN-GOD! (Hislop, page 222) For this reason God forbade it in Leviticus,

> Ye shall not round the corners of your heads; neither shalt thou mar the corners of thy beard. (Leviticus 19:27)

> They shall not make baldness upon their head, neither shall they shave off the corner of their beard, nor make any cuttings in their flesh. (Leviticus 21:5)

Besides a celibate priesthood, Semiramis developed a system of female devotees known as vestal virgins, later to be known by the Chaldean word, NUN, which means "Daughters of Nimrod" (Hislop, P. 223)

Their 'duty' in service to their 'god' Nimrod in this Babylonian priesthood was to 'sexually' serve the unmarried priests and monks since these men were not allowed to marry and have wives. This was seen as a form of worship to their god and kept the priests satisfied and happy in the priesthood, not to mention keeping them from turning homosexual. History attests to the horror of countless abortions which arose from this immoral system as countless bodies of babies have been found near convents and monasteries through out history. (See picture and details in Babylon Mystery Religion by Ralph Woodrow, pages 116,117) Many such gravesites for the aborted babies of these Nun/priest relationships were found in the underground tunnels between Convents and Monasteries in Spain and in Rome. By 1936, the citizens of Spain were so outraged because of this debauchery; they attacked and burnt many of the church buildings to the ground! (See Woodrow's book mentioned above). Nevertheless, forbidding the priests to marry resulted in much HOMOSEXUALITY among priests and the public allowed this immorality to continue to keep the priests away from their wives and daughters, according to Woodrow. To this day, history attests that the priesthood has proven a drawing net to homosexuals.

Semiramis claimed her Mystery Religion possessed the highest wisdom. It revealed divine secrets and those members of this religion would be the only ones to receive salvation to heaven after completing a series of religious works beginning with Baptism by the Babylonian Priest and ending with prayers for the dead. Hislop says these became known as Sacraments. Semiramis taught that devotees did not immediately enter heaven at death, but went to an intermediate place known as PURGATORY. (Hislop, p169) This held the family to remain faithful to the Babylonian Priesthood to assure their loved one could move on to heaven! Property and money could be donated to the Babylonian Priesthood and this would help get the one out of purgatory sooner. This later became known as 'Indulgences', according to Hislop.

The Old Testament informs us the spirit immediately returns to God who gave it at the death of the physical body. (Eccl. 12:6&7) And again in the New Testament, where it is given,

> We are confident, I say, and willing rather to be absent from the body, and to be present with the Lord. (2 Cor. 5:8)

The Priests also had control over the devotees because Semiramis compelled the people to confess to a Babylonian Priest at least once a year and to do penance according to the degree of the sins committed. Sins were categorized by their seriousness as either mortal or venial sins. Of course, none of this is in the Bible. The original purpose of the confessional was to keep tabs on any rebellion or uprising in the empire! This was effective because people were compelled to confess every sin, moral, ethical, whatever, to the priest. The omission of any sin could forfeit salvation! The problem of a celibate unmarried priesthood of males hearing the intimate private sexual confessions of married and single women eventually would lead to trouble as one would expect; and it did. A former Priest, Father Chiniquy, tells in his book THE PRIEST, THE WOMAN, & CONFESSIONAL, says that if married men and fathers knew the intimate questions that were asked of the wives and their daughters in the confessional booths, they would run the priests and their confessional booths out of town!! This book is also available from Chick Publications at the address above or www.chick.com.

Later on when the Babylonian Religion moved to Egypt, these priests imprinted the initials of Nimrod, Semiramis, and the son Tammuz on the wafer-cakes which were eaten, in a MASS CEREMONY, as the priest placed the wafer on the tongue of the person.

In the Egyptian language, Nimrod, Semiramis, and Tammuz were known as Seb, Isis, and Horus; thus IHS were imprinted on the wafer cakes. Many Christian churches still have this religious symbol of IHS on their church furniture and have no idea what it stands for!

Devotees of this Babylon Mystery Religion would make the mark of a 'T' with their hand across their chest in honor of Tammuz; later called genuflecting. We see this Tammuz being worshipped in the Old Testament times in Ezekiel 8:13, 14!

H.L. Willmington tells how this 'Babylon' Religion spread thru out the world and in the Old Testament became known as 'Baal' worship...(The King is Coming, p76) In Ezekiel, we read with the Lord speaking to Ezekiel:

> He said also unto me, Turn thee yet again, and thou shalt see greater abominations that they do. Then he brought me to the door of the gate of the LORD'S house which was toward the north; and, behold, there sat women weeping for Tammuz. (Ezekiel 8:13-14)

Starting to fit together? What was the teaching of Semiramis' Satanic Church? That Semiramis herself was the way to God. She actually adopted the title "Queen of Heaven."

We read about the worship of Semiramis and this Baal worship in Jeremiah,

> The children gather wood, and the fathers kindle the fire, and the women knead their dough, to make cakes to the queen of heaven, and to pour out drink offerings unto other gods, that they may provoke me to anger. (Jeremiah 7:18)

Notice this provokes God to anger!

> Thus saith the LORD of hosts, the God of Israel, saying; Ye and your wives have both spoken with your mouths, and fulfilled with your hand, saying, We will surely perform our vows that we have vowed, to burn incense to the queen of

heaven, and to pour out drink offerings unto her: ye will surely accomplish your vows, and surely perform your vows. (Jeremiah 44:25)

Adherents believed that she alone could administer salvation to the sinner through various sacraments, such as the sprinkling of holy water.

They believed that although her son Tammuz was tragically slain by a wild boar during a hunting trip; he was, however, resurrected from the dead forty days later. Thus, every year since the days of Tammuz, the temple virgins of this cult would enter a forty-day fast as a memorial to Tammuz' death and resurrection. This was later called 'LENT' (according to Hislop, author of "THE TWO BABYLONS")

Because of and based upon the prophecy stated in Genesis 3:15 of a coming Messiah, She now claimed she was CO-MEDIATRIX with her son.

LENT; which is observed for forty days, ending with Easter, is derived from the Babylonian system of mysteries. Perhaps you wondered why you never found the word mentioned in the Bible.

After the forty-day fast, a joyful feast called Ishtar (another name for Semiramis) took place. At this feast colored eggs were exchanged and eaten as a symbol of the resurrection. An evergreen tree was displayed and a Yule log was burned. Finally hot cakes marked with the letter T (to remind everybody of Tammuz) were baked and eaten.

This pagan festival of 'Ishtar' was celebrated hundreds of years before Christ, and it is even mentioned in Acts 12:3&4! The name has slightly changed to 'Easter'... One can see the resemblance - "Ishtar - Easter"

> And because he saw it pleased the Jews, he proceeded further to take Peter also. (Then were the days of unleavened bread.) And when he had apprehended him, he put him in prison, and delivered him to four quaternion of soldiers to keep him; intending after Easter to bring him forth to the people. (Acts 12:3-4)

The Greek word translated Easter comes from the Greek word "pascha" and means Passover.

The prophet Ezekiel was called by the Lord to go to the temple and see this cultic practice in process. Ezekiel stood watching the women of Israel observing the forty days of the Lent holidays. A holiday set aside for the slaying of the pagan, Tammuz. The Lord called this an abomination.

> He said also unto me, turn thee yet again, and thou shalt see greater abominations that they do. Then he brought me to the door of the gate of the LORD'S house which was toward the north; and, behold, there sat women weeping for Tammuz. (Ezekiel 8:13-14)

Here we see women weeping for Tammuz, whom Semiramis claimed was the 'resurrected' Nimrod! God calls it an abomination!

Thus, began the mother-child Cult which later spread all over the world. From the dispersion at Babel in Genesis 11, we see the Babylon Mystery Religion spread worldwide! From Babylon it spread to Phoenicia under the name of Ashteroth and

Tammuz. From Phoenicia, it traveled to Pergamos in Asia Minor. This is the reason for John's admonition to the church at Pergamos in the book of Revelation:

> I know thy works, and where thou dwellest, even where Satan's seat is . . ." (Rev. 2:13).

In Egypt the mother-child cult was known as Isis and Horus. In Greece it became Aphrodite and Eros. In Rome this pair was worshiped as Venus and cupid.

Clarence Larkin, in his classic, DISPENSATIONAL TRUTH, on page 140, traces this Babylon Mystery Religion down through history until it enters Rome:

"The city of Babylon continued to be the seat of Satan until the fall of the Babylonian and Medo-Persian Empires, when he shifted his Capital to Pergamos in Asia Minor, where it was in John's day. (Rev.2:12-13 see verse quoted above)

When Attalus, the Pontiff and King of Pergamos, died in B. C. 133, he bequeathed the Headship of the "Babylonian Priesthood" to Rome. When the Etruscans came to Italy from Lydia (the region of Pergamos), they brought with them the Babylonian religion and rites. They set up a Pontiff who was head of the Priesthood. Later the Romans accepted this Pontiff as their civil ruler. Julius Caesar was made Pontiff of the Etruscan Order in BC 74. In BC 63 he was made "Supreme Pontiff" of the "Babylonian Order," thus becoming heir to the rights and titles of Attalus, Pontiff of Pergamos, who had made Rome his heir by will. Thus, Julius Caesar, the first Roman Emperor became the Head of the "Babylonian Priesthood," and Rome became the successor to Babylon. The Emperors of Rome continued to exercise the office of "Supreme Pontiff" until A. D. 376, when the Emperor Gratian, for Christian reasons, refused it. The Bishop of the Church at Rome, Damasus, was elected to the position. He had been Bishop twelve years, having been made Bishop in A. D. 366, through the influence of the monks of Mt. Carmel, a college of Babylonian religion originally founded by the priests of Jezebel. So in A. D. 378 the Head of the "Babylonian Order" became the Ruler of the "Roman Church." Thus Satan united Rome and Babylon into One Religious System."

Soon after Damasus was made "Supreme Pontiff" the "rites" of Babylon began to come to the front. The worship of the Virgin Mary was set up in A. D. 381. (All the outstanding festivals of the Roman Catholic Church are of Babylonian origin.) Easter is not a Christian name. It means "Ishtar," one of the titles of the Babylonian Queen of Heaven, whose worship by the Children of Israel was such an abomination in the sight of God. The decree for the observance of Easter and Lent was given in A D 519.

The Catholic "Rosary" is of Pagan origin. There is no warrant in the Word of God for the use of the "Sign of the Cross." (It had its origin in the mystic "Tau" of the Chaldeans and Egyptians.) It came from the letter "T," the initial of the name "Tammuz," and was used in the "Babylonian Mysteries" for the same magic purposes as the Roman Catholic Church now employs it. Celibacy, the Tonsure, and the Order of Monks and

Nuns, have no warrant or authority from Scripture. The Nuns are nothing more than an imitation of the "Vestal Virgins" of Pagan Rome."

(The above taken from Clarence Larkin's DISPENSATIONAL TRUTH, page 140)

In the midst of all the growing of the "mystery Babylonian" religion, the Roman Emperor, Caesar Augustine has come to power; and has adopted Christianity as the official "religion" for the empire.

But to fully grasp what is and what will be taking place after Christ walked this earth and what we can expect in the future, we have to understand the vision given to Daniel of the Old Testament. Few understand what God has given us in this eleventh chapter of Daniel; but if you will bear with me, I think we'll come to grips with what God has related to us in his word.

The first verse of Daniel, chapter 11 reads,

> Also, I in the first year of Darius the Mede, even I, stood to confirm and to strengthen him. (Daniel 11:1)

This is Michael, the arch-angel speaking to Daniel after he has strengthened him. And he tells Daniel,

And now will I show thee the truth. Behold, there shall stand up yet three kings in Persia; and the fourth shall be far richer than they all: and by his strength through his riches he shall stir up all against the Grecia. (Daniel 11:2)

History records the succession of three kings in Persia and the last one was defeated by Alexander the Great, which is the "mighty King" spoken of in the next verse and the verse reads,

And a mighty king shall stand up, that shall rule with great dominion, and do according to his will. And when he shall stand up, his kingdom shall be broken, and shall be divided toward the four winds of heaven; and not to his posterity, nor according to his dominion which he ruled: for his kingdom shall be plucked up, even for others beside those. (Daniel 11:3-4)

We know from recorded history, Alexander conquered the known world and that he died at an early age with no heir to replace him. His kingdom was divided among his four Generals who took one part each of the North, South, East, and West parts of the empire. This is symbolized by the "four winds of heaven" in verse 4.

Continuing;

And the king of the south shall be strong, and one of his princes; and he (she) shall be strong above him, and have great dominion; his (her) dominion shall be a great dominion. (Daniel 11:5)

Hebrew, like in all the Mediterranean languages, the pronoun is dependent upon the usage in the sentence. For instance, in Spanish: la alumna, means student (girl), and el alumno, means student (boy); the difference between the meaning in the sentence of boy or girl is the ending placed on the words. This is also the case in the Hebrew language.

The Hebrew word translated "princes" comes from the Hebrew word "sar" and actually means "a head person of any rank or class" and in this case in the bible only one person in history fulfills this throne of the south.

This person in Daniel, Michael is referring to can be no other then Cleopatra, the powerful Queen of Egypt and a descendant of Alexander's General, Ptolemy. As stated in the next verse, Rome, under Julius Caesar, and Egypt, under Cleopatra, formed an alliance, but when Caesar was assassinated, Rome was divided in two camps with Mark Anthony going to Egypt and helping Cleopatra to fight against Rome. They lost and history hears nothing more of their posterity. As it is stated in the bible in Daniel,

> And in the end of years they shall join themselves together; for the king's daughter of the south shall come to the king of the north to make an agreement: but she shall not retain the power of the arm; neither shall he stand, nor his arm: but she shall be given up, and they that brought her, and he that begat her, and he that strengthened her in these times". (Daniel 11:6)

Finally, in 325 AD, the Nicene council is formed and all the different fractions of Christianity are invited to participate. The objective of this council was to decide once and for all times which of the current circulating writing were of God and which were of Man. The end result of this meeting was the bible we have today. A few of the old writings which were so popular at the time of the council meeting and were not canonized were left out of the "now canonized" sacred text.

It is at this time we see the seventh verse of Daniel, chapter eleven come into play. The verse reads,

> But out of a branch of her roots shall one stand up in his estate, which shall come with an army, and shall enter into the fortress of the king of the north, and shall deal against them, and shall prevail." (Daniel 11:7)

To get a better understanding of this verse, we have to ask ourselves, what are Cleopatra's roots? And the correct answer is the country of Greece. So it is in the nation of Greece where we'll find the prophecy of verse seven.

Three hundred years after Christ was crucified, a new empire was created in his name; that is Christianity. The new faith Rome had tried to stamp out was the force which brought Byzantium, the reorganized Roman Empire to survive for more than eleven hundred years. The idea of moving the Roman capital east was not something new; Julius Caesar in 45 BC considered moving the imperial capital somewhere else, either Alexander or Troy. Diocletian divided the empire in half and administered the eastern half from Nicomedia, which was near the town later called Constantinople. In 324 Constantine became sole ruler of the Empire and laid the foundation stone for the new city, Constantinople, of which became the new capital of the now called Byzantine Empire after Pope Leo III crowned Charles of the Franks as the Holy Roman Emperor. At this time if you can accept it, Christianity became King of the North. The Byzantine Empire, under the Christian flag conquered and reclaimed almost all of the old pagan

Rome's territories, including Egypt and most of North Africa. During this period, orthodox Christianity spread all the way into and throughout Russia.

Continuing: verse eight reads,

> And shall also carry captives into Egypt their gods, with their princes, and their precious vessels of silver and of gold; and he shall continue more years than the king of the north. (Daniel 11:8)

This verse is a little hard to understand; but, remember Mohammed was born and the religion of Islam begins to flourish beginning about six hundred thirty AD. This religion spread to Egypt and North Africa and its leaders became quite wealthy under their form of government. Islam became the religion of the Ottoman Empire which ruled basically most of Asia Minor. I think it safe to say this religion is to be considered the king of the south because it spread from Arabia to India going east and all the way to Spain going west at its height. The next verse deals with the demise of the empire and Islamic culture.

Verse 9 reads,

> So, the king of the south shall come into his kingdom, and shall return into his own land". (Daniel 11:9)

The next few verses are probably speaking of Genghis Khan and his hordes. He conquered everything south of the "Pillars of Hercules" and could have gone into Europe, but history tells us he never mastered the art of making firearms, canons, and etc. which he was told the Europeans possessed. History records Genghis Khan refused to invade Europe because he feared defeat without these new weapons of war.

The rest of this chapter is left to conjecture and many peoples in the modern world could possibly fit; but history will finally show what is what. We will leave this part of history and continue with the events before Christ will appear again to take over his kingdom.

Even though Christianity is officially the religion of the Byzantine and Frankish Empires, there are a lot of fractions existing within the Christian sect. The most notable ones were the Arians, the Semi-Arians, the Nicaeans, and the Cappadocians.

The Arians believed God the Father and God the Son are dissimilar in essence. The son is divine but not fully divine. Because the son was begotten by the Father, there must have been a time when the Son didn't exist. The Son is subject to the Father, and the Holy Spirit is subject to the Son. Arianism was outlawed in 381 AD at the council of Constantinople but continued to flourish in the West part of the Empire for the next four hundred years.

The Simi-Arians believed the Son is similar to the Father but not in all things. He is not a creature of God in the way angels and mankind are defined as "creatures". The semi-Arians remained influential until the 381 AD council of Constantinople.

The Nicaeans believed the Father and the Son are of identical substance with each other. The Son must have full divinity in order to vanquish evil and save sinners. The Nicaean party was vindicated at Constantinople in 381 AD and again at the Council of Chalcedon in 451 AD. Their Nicene creed has been a basic article of faith for Christians ever sense.

The Cappadocians believed that God the Father and God the Son were of identical substance; but they also emphasized that the Father and Son were distinct, though equally divine, hence of like substance.

It is well to add here the views given above are not in line with Biblical scriptures. Christ said,

> Have I been so long time with you, and yet hast thou not known me, Phillip? He that hath seen me hath seen the Father; how sayest thou then, show us the Father? (John 14:9)

Christ is reminding Phillip that He and God are one and the same. As we continue with Christ's dialogue to Phillip, we see this to be the essence of his teaching,

> Believest thou not that I am in the Father, and the Father in me? The words that I speak unto you I speak not of myself: but the Father that dwelleth in me, he doeth the works. (John 14:10)

What is inside this physical body? We all know we have a spirit of one of his children created in the first earth age residing inside this physical body. And so residing inside the physical body of Christ was the Holy Spirit of God, himself. Further evidence

is shown in the book of John where it is written,

> In the beginning was the Word, and the Word was with God, and the Word was
> God. (John 1:1)

We have another witness in the Book of Revelation if you can grasp it. In chapter

five of Revelation, we have John speaking with an elder because he was weeping

concerning the fact no one in heaven or earth or under the earth was found worthy to

open the book with seven seals holding it closed. The elder tells John not to worry

because the Lion of the tribe of Judah, the Root of David will open the book and loose

the seven seals. And John sees and,

> And I beheld, and lo, in the midst of the throne and of the four beasts, and in the
> midst of the elders, stood a lamb as it had been slain, having seven horns and
> seven eyes, which are the seven spirits of God sent forth into all the earth. And he
> came and took the book out of the right hand of him that sat upon the throne.
> (Rev. 5:5-7)

At first glance, we seem to be dealing with two separate deities, but on closer

scrutiny, we readily understand there is only one deity on this scene. Perhaps, two

different offices of the same Lord is shown here. Why do I say this you might wonder?

Look at the last verse of chapter four in Revelation and it reads,

> Thou art worthy, O Lord, to receive glory and honour and power; for thou hast
> created all things, and for thy pleasure they are and were created. (Rev. 4:11)

But we have this same statement given about Christ in the book of Colossians where Paul is giving thanks to God for his Son, and we read,

> Who is the image of the invisible God, the firstborn of every creature: for by him were all things created, that are in heaven, and that are in earth, visible, and invisible, whether they be thrones, or dominions, or principalities, or powers: all things were created by him, and for him. (Colossians 1:15-16)

So, you see at first glance, it looks like the same credit is given to God the Father and to God the Son and this is correct because they are one and the same, only two different offices or roles they are fulfilling.

And again, in the book of Isaiah we read,

> I am the Lord, and there is none else, there is no God beside me: I girded thee, though thou have not known me: (Isaiah 45:5)

And again, for emphasis,

> Tell ye, and bring them near; yea, let them take counsel together: who hath declared this from ancient time? Who hath told it from that time? Have not I the Lord? And there is no God else beside me; a just God and a savior; there is none beside me. Look unto me, and be ye saved, all the ends of the earth: for I am God, and there is none else. I have sworn by myself; the word is gone out of my mouth in righteousness, and shall not return, that unto me every knee shall bow, every tongue shall swear". (Isaiah 45:21-23)

If I haven't made myself clear on this subject, let me say this; God being a spirit can encompass the entire earth similar to the air we breathe. As water can be separated into different places and still keep all of its chemical properties, God can and did enter into the Virgin Mary, causing her to be pregnant and also entered the unborn fetus that was to become Jesus of Nazareth. We all know we have a spirit placed in our bodies from God which is only released at the death of the physical body. God did the same with Jesus, except he placed his own spirit into Jesus which was released at his death on the cross. Satan knew this and believed he could kill God while he was in the flesh body; that is the reason he tried to discredit Jesus so often and eventually caused his death on the cross. What Satan may not have realized was that he sealed his own death warrant by committing this murder. This is one of the reasons Christ told his disciples.

If you have seen me, you have seen the Father. (John 14:9)

He was housing the Father in his flesh body.

Now, getting back to our subject of the Kingdom being postponed; as the centuries rolled by, the Catholic Church gained the most ground. They assimilated the "mystery religion" started by Nimrod and used their ideas of Cardinals, and bishops, and other figures to go with their idea of Christianity. They call the twenty-fifth of December, Christ's birthday to blend with Pagan worship. The name of Passover was changed to Easter because it fell close to the spring equinox and pagan holidays. This mixing was easier to bring new converts from paganism into Christianity then disallowing pagan participation and shunning the pagan's old gods.

Starting in the fifteen century, we have the beginning of the protestant reformation starting. In 1517, Martin Luther issued his "Ninety-Five Theses" in a letter to several bishops, hoping to spark debate. John Calvin and others further criticized Catholic teachings. In Germany, the reformation led to war between the Protestant Schmalkaldic League and the Catholic Emperor Charles V. In France, a series of conflicts termed the French Wars of Religion was fought from 1562 to 1598 between the Huguenots and the forces of the French Catholic League.

Popes have always pushed the link between the Virgin Mary as Mother of God and the full acceptance of Jesus Christ as Son of God. In the nineteen century, they were highly important for the development of "Mariology" to explain the veneration (veneration = worship, adore, revere) of Mary through their decisions not only in the area of Marian beliefs, but also Marian practices and devotions. Before the nineteenth century, Popes promulgated Marian veneration by authorizing new Marian feast days, prayers, initiatives, the acceptance and support of Marian congregations. Pope Pius XII also promulgated the new feast Queenship of Mary celebrating Mary as "Queen of Heaven" and he introduced the first ever Marian year in 1954, a second one was proclaimed by Pope John Paul II. Pope Pius, IX. Pope Pius XI and Pope Pius XII facilitated the veneration (worship) of Marian apparitions such as in Lourdes and Fatima. Later Popes such as John XXIII to Benedict XVI promoted the visits to Marian shrines (Benedict XVI in 2007 and 2008). The second Vatican Council highlighted the importance of Marian veneration (worship) in "Lumen Gentium". During the Council, Pope Paul VI proclaimed Mary to be the "Mother of the Church".

Does any of the above paragraph sound familiar? I believe we covered this same type earlier in the Pagan religion of Tammuz and his mother which God spoke against in the Book of Ezekiel. (Ezekiel 8:14-17 and also in Jeremiah 44:17-19) We know the ancient "mystery religion" was one of Satan's doing; but now we see the same type of origination calling itself "Christian" and Christ in the place of "Tammuz" and Mary as the "Queen of Heaven". What is the old saying, "A rose by any other name is still as rose"? It's no wonder there are so many atrocities being brought to light in the "Catholic Church".

Perhaps, now you will begin to understand, Satan has a master plan the same as our Father; but Satan's plan is to set himself up as the "Christ" and to be worshipped as Christ. This information is given by Paul in the second book of Thessalonians where Paul is answering questions about when the return of Christ would take place. Keeping this thought in mind, we read,

> Let no man deceive you by any means: for that day shall not come, except there come a falling away first, and that man of sin be revealed, the son of perdition: who opposeth and exalteth himself above all that is called God, or that is worshipped; so that he as God sitteth in the temple of God, shewing himself that he is God. (2 Thessalonians 1:3-4)

Well, we have a great "falling away" from the true church these days. We have "evolution" taught in the schools and God's word replaced by science. And people wonder why the kids in school are fighting and killing among themselves. We are waiting for that "man of sin" to reveal himself; but who is this man of sin? Scanning the whole written word of God, we find only one individual by name who has been condemned to death. Are you surprised at this, to find only one person God has sentenced to death; to be totally erased from existence. Maybe, before I give you his name, we should have a better understanding of what God considers "sin". We can find the definition in the book of 1 John where it is stated,

> Whosoever committeth sin transgresseth also the law: for sin is the transgression of the law. (1 John 3:4)

Now then, God's law is given to us in the form of the 10 commandments located in Exodus, chapter 20 starting with verse 3 and ending with verse 17.

Now that you know the rules of life, we can fathom the need for Jesus Christ to come into this flesh world; because we can still have life by accepting his sacrifice, and depending on his righteous to come before our Heavenly Father with our sins covered by the blood of Christ who loved us enough to pay our sin debt, and give us a ticket into Heaven, and the joy of sharing all the Father has for his children. All we have to do is accept this gift from our Heavenly Father and repent of the sins committed; then live the best we can in the way Christ would be pleased. If we do this, we will live because our debt of sin has been paid by Jesus; if we refuse this gift from Christ that he gave for us, we are "dead men walking".

Satan would not accept this; instead he led God's children and his brothers into a war against God and tried to set himself on the very throne of God. Pride was his downfall; he began to think of himself as being better then God and more powerful and his way of doing things was better then God's way of doing things. What will eventually happen to Satan and his pride? We are told in the book of Ezekiel what the Devil has coming to him. We'll begin our reading with Ezekiel 28, verse 12. In this chapter Satan is called the "king of Tyrus" and when you translate "tyrus" from the Hebrew, it means "rock", but he's not our rock; our Rock is Christ. Satan has always tried to imitate Christ and this will be part of his deception when he returns to earth shortly.

In Ezekiel, we read,

> Son of man, take up a lamentation upon the King of Tyrus, and say unto him, thus saith the Lord God; thou sealest up the sum, full of wisdom, and perfect in beauty. Thou hast been in Eden the garden of God; every precious stone was thy covering, the sardius, topaz, and the diamond, the beryl, the onyx, and the jasper, the sapphire, the emerald, and the carbuncle, and gold: the workmanship of thy tabrets and of thy pipes was prepared in thee in the day thou wast created. (Ezekiel 28:12-13)

Notice Satan was created and nothing was spared to make him perfect in mind and body. All the precious stones and such are symbols for us to understand Satan was given the best of everything. The reference to Eden is given so we will know without a doubt; Satan was the serpent or the tree of knowledge of good and evil who brought about Adam and Eve's downfall. Now, continuing,

> Thou are the anointed cherub that covereth; and I have set thee so; thou wast upon the holy mountain of God; thou hast walked up and down in the midst of the stones of fire. Thou wast perfect in thy ways from the day that thou wast created, till iniquity was found in thee. (Ezekiel 28:14-15)

Satan didn't start out bad; he was given this earth to rule by God's standards, but he blew it. He was supposed to protect the mercy seat; the very seat of total power, but he wanted to sit on it instead. He was hailed by the rest of God's children as a wonderful ruler at first. How long he ruled this way is not told; perhaps, a few million years or only days; but he let his pride in himself turn his thoughts to jealousy. He wanted to be God!

Continuing,

> By the multitude of thy merchandise they have filled the midst of thee with violence, and thou hast sinned: therefore, I will cast thee as profane out of the mountain of God: and I will destroy thee, O covering Cherub, from the midst of the stones of fire. Thine heart was lifted up because of thy beauty, thou hast corrupted thy wisdom by reason of thy brightness: I will cast thee to the ground, and I lay thee before kings, that they may behold thee. (Ezekiel 28:16-17)

Kicking Satan out of the mountain of God means he will be removed from heaven because he "sinned" and he is told why this is going to happen to him; in other words, his mind became filled with thoughts and an attitude contrary to God's way of doing things. Perhaps your parents had a similar saying. My parent's rules were "it's my way or the highway" and so it was with God. Next, we'll read how God is going to destroy Satan.

And we read,

> Thou hast defiled thy sanctuaries by the multitude of thine iniquities, by the iniquity of thy traffick; therefore will I bring forth a fire from the midst of thee, it shall devour thee, and I will bring thee to ashes upon the earth in the sight of all them that behold thee. All they that know thee among the people shall be astonished at thee: thou shall be a terror, and never shalt thou be anymore. (Ezekiel 28:18-19)

For a better understanding of this last paragraph, we have to realize Satan is a solid supernatural being and as Christ stated, God is Spirit. Also, in Hebrews, we are told in chapter 12, verse 29 that "our God is a consuming fire". And this "Fire" will enter Satan and destroy him; he will be burnt until nothing is left but ashes which will blow away in the wind until everything including the memory of him is forgotten.

So, maybe now any misunderstanding about the "son of Perdition" will be clear. It is not Judas Iscariot as some have taught. When you search the scriptures, Judas repented of his sin and returned the 30 pieces of silver and repented of his deed and he was forgiven as Christ has promised all who repent. (Matt. 27:3-5)

So now, we wait: Christ gave us a timetable of the events we are to expect to happen before his return. They are given in four places in the bible; so Christ considered them important and so must we. These events are given in Matthew, chapter 24; in Mark, chapter 13; in Luke, chapter 21; and finally, in the book of Revelation. They are all the same; maybe, one or the other is easier to understand.

Basically, from Mark, chapter 13, we have these things to happen: Christ said,

> For many shall come in my name, saying, I am Christ; and shall deceive many.
> (Mark 13:6)

This has been happening since the first century and still goes on today. Of lately, one of the more infamous ones was Jim Jones, the founder of The People's Temple and who in 1978 led his followers to Jamestown, Guyana where they under went a mass suicide

and over 900 Temple members died.

> And when ye shall hear of wars and rumors of wars, be ye not troubled: for such things must needs be; but the end shall not be yet. For nation shall rise against nation, and kingdom against kingdom: and there shall be earthquakes in various places, and there shall be famines and troubles: these are the beginning of sorrows. (Mark 13:7-8)

Wars and rumors of war and earthquakes have been in ever century since Christ

walked the earth in the flesh.

> But take heed to yourselves: for they shall deliver you up to councils; and in the synagogues ye shall be beaten: and ye shall be brought before rulers and kings for my sake, for a testimony against them. And the gospel must first be published among all nations. (Mark 13:9-10)

Christians have been prosecuted in every country on earth at one time or the other.

And now, in this time of the 21st century, this gospel of Christ has been preached in all

the Nations. So, we are right at the threshold of the next big event to take place on earth.

What is this big event; it is the coming of Satan posing as the returned Christ.

Christ said,

> But when ye shall see the ABOMINATION OF THE DESOLATOR, spoken of by Daniel the prophet, standing where he ought not, (let him that reads understand,) then let them that be in Judaea flee to the mountains: and let him that is on the housetop not go down into the house, neither enter therein, to take any thing out of his house: and let him that is in the field not turn back again for to take up his garment. (Mark 13:14-16)

The idea of this verse is that when Satan sits on the throne of the world in Jerusalem as his capital city, the return of the real Christ is imminent. His return will be so swift, a person won't have time to stop his work and grab a jacket or leave his place of work to prepare for the real Christ. The complete meaning is for you to be prepared for the real Christ's return at all times because you can tell the difference between the real and the fake.

I've written lengthy commentaries on this subject in my book "A Path thru the Weeds", so I won't tire you out by giving this lesson again. I will say this; we are in the fifth trump and close to the end of it. The next major thing to watch for happens in the sixth trump and it is the coming of Satan to rule the earth.

How will he arrive or what causes him to come to the earth in person? Well, we know Satan is located behind Christ who is at the right hand of God at present because that is where Christ told him to go. (Luke 4:8); but pretty soon in the war going on in heaven, Satan and his allies will be tossed out onto the earth as it is recorded in Revelation, and it reads,

> And there was war in heaven: Michael and his angels fought against the dragon; and the dragon fought and his angels, and prevailed not; neither was their place found any more in heaven. And the great dragon was cast out, that old serpent, called the Devil, and Satan, which deceives the whole world: he was cast out into the earth, and his angels were cast out with him. (Rev. 12:7-9)

Oh, don't be worried, Satan's not coming as a bad guy. He's coming as a good guy, and he will be calling himself, "The Christ". He's going to bring peace to the world and fix everybody's problems; or so he thinks. Maybe, I shouldn't have said for you not to be worried because if you follow this imitation of Christ, Christ will be mad and if you don't Satan will be mad. So, you'll make somebody angry; your choice? Anyway, this deception Satan tries to use to pull the "wool over the eyes" of God's children will cause God to act and he will send the real Christ to take charge. (Matt. 25:31)

Do you know when he will come; this man who will claim to be Christ; this son of God who we call Satan or the Devil? In the book of 2 Peter, we are told by Peter the day of the Lord or the day when Christ will come will be like a thief in the night. And he says the "heavens shall pass away with a great noise, and the elements shall melt with fervent heat, the earth also, and the works that are therein shall be burned up". (2 Peter 3:10) This verse scares a lot of people because of the way it has been translated from the Greek.

What Peter is saying is that when Christ returns, everybody will be changed into spiritual bodies and all flesh and all things which offend God will be destroyed. We will start the Millennium fresh with God's Elect keeping order and teaching everybody the right way to please God. The hidden dynasties, or better said, the kings of the earth will no longer control the events of the world. In case you didn't know, the kings of the earth are Financial, political, education, and religion. (1 Cor. 15:51-54)

Part Four

The Second Advent: The first resurrection.

When Christ returns, he's not coming as a meek, easy going savior like he did the

first time; he's coming as an avenging warrior to take charge of his kingdom. And, he

will destroy all things in it which offend him. This idea is given in several places in the

bible but we can read about one statement in the parable of the ten talents, and we read,

> But those mine enemies which would not that I reign over them, bring hither, and
> slay them before me. (Luke 19:27)

One of those enemies is Satan and this is the sentence Christ gives him as recorded

in the book of Revelation, and it reads,

> And I saw an angel come down from heaven, having the key of the bottomless pit
> and a great chain in his hand. And he laid hold on the dragon, that old serpent,
> which is the Devil, and Satan, and bound him a thousand years, and cast him into
> the bottomless pit, and shut him up, and set a seal upon him, that he should
> deceive the nations no more, till the thousand years should be fulfilled: and after
> that he must be loosed a little season. (Rev. 20:1-3)

Just as much as the bible teaches us the love of Christ and the way we are supposed

to live in order to please him, the bible also teaches us what it's going to be like when he

returns. A lot of this information is given in parables, but enough is given in plain language so there will be no excuse for your actions when the Holy King Christ comes.

Did you notice the title I gave Christ? I didn't just pick it out of the air, it's recorded in

the book of Revelation and it reads,

> And he hath on his vesture and on his thigh a name written, KING OF KINGS,
> AND LORD OF LORDS. (Rev. 19:16)

Have you started to grasp the meaning of this tile? Christ will have the final say in all

things; life or death is his to grant or take away. We have had examples of this type of

government before in the Old Testament and there are still a few countries which seat a

monarch on a throne, but most of the monarchs don't have total authority anymore

because they misused their power. They were given this power to rule their people justly,

but all wound up using this power for selfish reasons and their subjects rebelled and some

of the Kings or Queens were executed for their wrongs. In this country of America, we

just vote them out of office or maybe a misguided fool will assassinate the public official.

So, in America, we'll have to learn how to give due homage to our King. There's nothing

to worry about really because Christ will rule justly and remember, he reads minds. You

won't be able to lie your way out of a predicament or jam you have gotten into. Cheer up!

It won't be bad because when you are changed into a spiritual body, you'll also get a

mind that remembers all things and the ways of Christ will be a good way. Christ said, "If

ye love me, keep my commandments." (John 14:15) We like Christ being our savior and

removing sin off the book of life where our names are listed. But, it's a different thing to

start thinking of Christ as being solely in charge and having to obey everything he says.

This is the problem Satan has; he doesn't want to take orders from God or Christ of anybody! He thinks he knows best and he believes the world should do as he says. Have you though about how like Satan we really are? What about your teenage children; aren't they just treading water until they can get out from under Mon and Dad's guide lines and do as they please?

With these thoughts in mind, what can we expect to take place when Christ returns to take charge of his Kingdom? We can find these answers and all answers in God's Holy Word; for Christ told us in the book of Mark, "But take ye heed: behold, I have foretold you all things." (Mark 13:23) This makes it simple, doesn't it? All we have to do is study our bibles and we will know what to expect when Christ returns. Great; right? The key word is 'we have to study', and not somebody else doing the studying and telling you what the bible instructs. We can't do that because it's like somebody else doing your homework. When you are called on for an answer from the Master, how will you know for sure you can give the right answer unless you have completed the lesson assignment yourself? It would be alright to get a little help on parts you can't comprehend, but make sure the help comes from the right place and double check the sources.

We're going to start with the book of Isaiah and the prophecies to get an understanding of what's in the mind of God for Christ to correct at his second coming. The prophet writes,

> The lofty looks of man shall be humbled, and the haughtiness of men shall be bowed down, and the Lord alone shall be exalted in that day. (Isaiah 2:9)

What day is the prophet talking about? It's the day of the Lord or we could say the Millennium which lasts for a thousand years of our time.

The "lofty" looks could be described as "one-up-manship" or "pride" in yourself in today's language. It's the pride you take in all the material possessions acquired by "hook or crook" in today's world. It's looking down your nose at a less fortunate child of God, and belittling their efforts to fit into society. The "good o' boy" system will be done away. Don't take what I'm saying wrong; God loves for people to be rich with material possession. He just wants you to have earned your riches and use them in the right manner. Perhaps, you really don't know the right manner; so, let God's word help you and we see,

> Let him that stole steal no more; but rather let him labor, working with his hands the thing which is good, that he may have to give to him that needed. (Ephesians 4:28)

We need to give God the glory for every good thing which happens to us and to always remember the blessings he gives can just as easily be taken away if or when we stop being pleasing to him. Did you catch the end part of this verse above, the part which says, "To give to him that needed"?

The next few passages of Isaiah tell it pretty straight:

> For the day of the Lord of Hosts shall be upon everyone that is proud and lofty, and upon everyone that is lifted up; and he shall be brought low: and upon all the cedars of Lebanon, that are high and lifted up, and upon all the oaks of Bashan, and upon all the hills that are lifted up, and upon every tower, and upon every fenced wall, and upon all the ships of Tarshish, and upon all pleasant pictures. And the loftiness of man shall be bowed down, and the haughtiness of men shall be made low: and the Lord alone shall be exalted in that day. And the idols he shall utterly abolish. (Isaiah 2:12-18)

The "cedars of Lebanon" and the "oaks of Bashan" were the biggest and best trees in that part of the world; they were similar to the "redwoods" of California today. The similarities are to men who consider themselves the same. Towers and fenced walls and hills are means of keeping people out and defending your ill gotten wealth instead of depending on God and his wisdom for protection. When the Lord returns, every knee will bow and every person will be in submission to Christ. (Isaiah 45:23) And also in the book of Romans, it reads,

> For it is written, as I live, said the Lord, every knee shall bow to me, and every tongue shall confess to God. (Romans 14:11)

The "ships of Tarshish" refer to large ocean-going vessels first mentioned in 1 Kings 10:22 during Solomon's reign. They hauled vast qualities of gold, silver, ivory, apes, and peacocks to King Hiram of Tyre. The ships put in to a port at a "rock" or island a short way off the coast of Tyre which the Kenites had fortified strongly against any kind of attacks from wandering thieves or conquering hordes. They had a strong trade going in this place and overcharged for goods going and coming. So, in history, "ships of Tarshish" became known as ill-gotten gains or selfish wealth. Tyre translates from

Hebrew to English as "rock" and this place and the deceptive trading practices on this site

is the reason Ezekiel uses the name in referring to Satan and his downfall.

We have a description of the events taking place at the start of the day of the Lord in

Zechariah, chapter 14. Beginning with verse 2, we read,

> Behold, the day of the Lord comes, and thy spoil shall be divided in the midst of thee. For I will gather all nations against Jerusalem to battle; and the city shall be taken, and the houses rifled, and the women ravished; and the half of the city shall go forth into captivity, and the residue of the people shall not be cut off from the city. (Zech. 14:2)

As we learned earlier, Satan is sitting on his throne in Jerusalem claiming to be Jesus

and running the one world political camp, only it's not working out like it should have by

all the promises he made to get control of all the governments of the world. It sounds like

the politicians of today doesn't it? God will sow seeds of unrest among all the nations so

that they will come up against Jerusalem to destroy Satan and all his "fallen angels" who

have been helping him. As total chaos starts to develop on all the earth and Jerusalem is

under siege, Then God will send the real Christ to take charge.

Next verse reads,

> Then shall the Lord go forth, and fight against those nations, as when he fought in the day of battle. And his feet shall stand in that day upon the mount of Olives, which is before Jerusalem on the east, and the mount of Olives shall cleave in the midst thereof toward the east and toward the west, and there shall be a very great valley; and half of the mountain shall remove toward the north and half of it toward the south. (Zech. 14:3-4)

After Christ arrives, there will be a very short battle and Christ will seat himself on his throne. The throne God promised David that would be occupied by a descendant of his flesh body until the rightful King came to claim it. That King is Jesus Christ.

> And it shall come to pass in that day, said the Lord of Hosts, that I will cut off the names of the idols out of the land, and they shall no more be remembered: and also I will cause the prophets and the unclean spirit to pass out of the land. (Zechariah 13:2)

Christ will rid the world of anything evil or offensive to him. He will set up his throne on Mt Zion and will conduct his government from there. A lot of misguided Christians are looking forward to this "Day of the Lord" so they can talk to Christ and give him a hug. It's not going to happen at first when he arrives. It will not happen until the thousand years reign is over and Satan has been disposed of. Why? Remember the Father will not touch or look on any thing evil or unclean; so, in essence, until everybody has a full knowledge of God's plan for their life and they accept it with joy, they will not be allowed to come into contact with Christ. At the end of the thousand-year reign, Satan will be loosed a little while to try God's people and try to deceive them into following him again. Surprisingly, a large number will still follow Satan knowing full well God's plan and how his Kingdom will operate. The bible says they will follow Satan right into the "Lake of Fire" and be destroyed forever along with Satan.

But let's read how the bible puts this sad time in the lives of some of God's children. It says,

> But the rest of the dead (this means everybody who didn't make it in the first resurrection) lived not again (meaning didn't have eternal life in them; only a spiritual body) until the thousand years were finished. This is the first resurrection. Blessed and holy is he that hath part in the first resurrection: on such the second death (this is the death of the spiritual body given when Christ first arrived on earth to take charge of his Kingdom and also the soul, spirit; everything which is you) hath no power, but they shall be priests of God and of Christ, and they shall reign with him a thousand years. And when the thousand years are expired, Satan shall be loosed out of his prison, and shall go out to deceive the nations which are in the four quarters of the earth, (meaning all over the whole earth) Gog and Magog to gather them together to battle: the number of whom is as the sand of the sea. And they went up the breath of the earth, (means, they came from everywhere) and compassed the camp of the saints about, and the beloved city: and fire came down from God out of heaven, and devoured them. And the devil that deceived them was cast into the lake of fire and brimstone, where the beast and false prophet are, (beast and false prophet are not people but symbolizes evil dictators and pagan religion) and shall be tormented day and night forever and ever. (Rev. 20:5-10; emphases mine)

You need to understand, the word devil, given above is not "the Devil". He has

already been destroyed along with all who rebelled and surrounded the camp of the saints

as stated above. The term "devil" is only the office Satan held. It is the office of lies and

deception and evil which is completely done away and like the false prophet and beast,

we won't have to deal with these things or thoughts again, ever.

Even the ones who serve Christ will not be allowed to bring anything unclean into

the presence of Christ as it is recorded in the book of Ezekiel, and we read,

> But the priests the Levites, the sons of Zadok, that kept the charge of my sanctuary when the children of Israel went astray from me, they shall come near to me to minister unto me, and they shall stand before me to offer unto me the fat and the blood, saith the Lord God: they shall enter into my sanctuary, and they shall come near to my table to minister unto me, and they shall keep my charge. And it shall come to pass, that when they enter in at the gates of the inner court,

they shall be clothed with linen garments; and no wool shall come upon them, whiles they minister in the gates of the inner court, and within. They shall have linen bonnets upon their heads, and shall have linen breeches upon their loins; they shall not gird themselves with anything that causes sweat. And when they go forth into the outer court, even into the outer court to the people, they shall put off their garments wherein they ministered, and lay them in the holy chambers, and they shall put on other garments; and they shall not sanctify the people with their garments. (Ezekiel 44:15-19).

So, you see, at the beginning of the Millennium, nobody but the Elect of God will come into contact with Christ. Only those people who have been tried and justified by God will he use to minister to Christ. Which brings me to who and what constitutes an Elect of God. The first mention of God having an Election is given in Isaiah and the prophet is stating God's words for the future Messiah, but let's read together what the bible says,

> Behold my servant, (Christ) whom I uphold; mine "elect", in whom my soul delighted; I have put my spirit upon him: he shall bring forth judgment to the Gentiles. (Isaiah 42:1; emphases mine)

In this case, God is describing the duties Christ will perform; that is, the office of Messiah has always been with God from the very beginning and at the "set" time that office will be brought forth to do its job. (John 1:1)

The Nation of Israel is also the elect of God; now then, I'm not talking about the modern nation of Israel, but the real Nation of Israel. The nation which God has scattered throughout this earth and only God knows where all of them are. They are the election of

God because of Jacob. (Isaiah 45:4) Also again in the book of Isaiah, speaking of the coming Christ, we read,

> And I will bring forth a seed out of Jacob, and out of Judah an inheritor of my mountains: and mine elect shall inherit it, and my servants shall dwell there. (Isaiah 45:4)

God's elect are first mentioned in the New Testament in the book of Matthew in chapter 24. Christ is doing the talking so we know he is describing other people and he says,

> And except those days should be shortened, there should no flesh be saved: but for the elect's sake those days shall be shortened. Then if any man shall say unto you, lo, here is Christ, or there, believe it not. For there shall arise false Christs, and false prophets, and shall show great signs and wonders; insomuch that, if it were possible, they shall deceive the very "elect. (Matt. 24:22)

In these passages, Christ is describing the events which are to happen at the end of this age. He's telling of the days while Satan is on the throne of God and claiming to be "The Christ".

There are enough passages in the bible for you to accept God has an election; but what is this election all about and why are they in the world? We will try to give an understanding of what the election is about first, and then we'll try to give an understanding of who the Elect are. To start with, God is not all knowing as a lot of preacher's teach and preach. If he were, there would have been no need for this physical earth age. God would have just destroyed all the ones who didn't love him and followed

Satan in the first rebellion of the first earth age. He has given most freewill; the freedom to love him or reject him and his kingdom. God does read minds and knows your thoughts, but he doesn't interfere with the ones who have freewill unless you ask him for help. Which brings us to the Elect of God, they don't have freewill. They are here to be used by God as he see fit. No? You have trouble accepting this concept? What did God say about Jeremiah? In the first chapter of Jeremiah, we read,

> Then the word of the Lord came unto me, saying, before I formed thee in the belly I knew thee; and before thou came forth out of the womb I sanctified thee, and I ordained thee a prophet unto the Nations. (Jeremiah 1:5)

How did God know Jeremiah? It could only be what he did in the first earth age. There are others, but let's look at the New Testament and the calling of Paul the apostle. We read,

> But the Lord said unto him, go thy way: for he is a chosen vessel unto me, to bear my name before the Gentiles, and kings, and the children of Israel: for I must show him how great things he must suffer for my name's sake. (Acts 9:15-16)

And, of course all the Disciples of Christ are of the "elect". All Christ had to say to them was, "Come follow me", and they left all and followed him, some eventually being killed for following him. (Matt. 4:19) And then there is the case of Jacob and Esau; God said he loved Jacob, but hated Esau. He said he hated Esau even before he was born. We are told in the scriptures that God is not a respecter of persons, so how could he hate Esau before he was born and had not done anything right or wrong in his life? The bible tells us,

For the children being not yet born, neither having done any good or evil, that the purpose of God according to election might stand, not of works but of him that calls; it is said unto her, the elder shall serve the younger. As it is written, Jacob have I loved, but Esau have I hated. (Romans 9:11-13)

Where is it written in the Old Testament these words quoted by Paul in the previous verse? It is written in the book of Malachi and it reads,

I have loved you, said the Lord. Yet ye say, wherein have thou loved us? Was not Esau Jacob's brother, said the Lord: yet I loved Jacob, and I hated Esau, and laid his mountains and his heritage waste for the dragons of the wilderness? (Malachi 1:2-3)

Why would God hate an unborn child? The apostle Paul asks the same basic question; was God unrighteous, and the answer was, No! So, there has to be another reason and it could only be because of the way Esau lived and loved in the first earth age before God changed all of his children into spirits, and brought them into this second earth age in physical form. (Psalm 104:4)

So now maybe you are starting to see the work and job which God uses his Election to accomplish. As Paul writes in the book of Ephesians in his introduction of the epistle,

According as he hath chosen us in him before the foundation of the world, that we should be holy and without blame before him in love: having predestinated us unto the adoption of children by Jesus Christ to himself, according to the good pleasure of his will, to the praise of the glory of his grace, wherein he hath made us accepted in the beloved. (Eph. 1:4-6)

Some were chosen by God before the overthrow of Satan's government on earth. This word "foundation" used above is translated from the Greek word "Katabole" and means a deposition; that is, an opposition to what's happening; it is derived from the Greek word "Kataballo", meaning to throw down. The idea is that something has been thrown away or overthrown. Paul states God chose his election before this government of Satan was overthrown. So, we can only conclude they were chosen because they stood in opposition of Satan and his allies. These are the ones God has "justified" (already judged) and now, in this earth age can be used of God to do the business of God. This is the reason God tells us not to judge. We don't know who the elect are and what their missions are. Only God knows who the elect are. He gives us rules to judge men by and we are to leave the rest up to him.

As Paul writes in Romans,

> And we know all things work together for good to them that love God, to them who are "the called" according to his purpose. For whom he did foreknow, (knew beforehand; that is in the first earth age) he also did predestinate to be conformed to the image of his Son, that he might be the firstborn among many brethren. Moreover whom he did predestinate, them he also called: and whom he called, them he also justified: (already judged) and whom he justified, them he also glorified. (Romans 8:28-31; emphases mine)

And also,

> Who shall lay anything to the charge of God's elect? It is God that justified. (Romans 8:33)

Second. God does not see into the future. He's not a time-traveler, but he makes the future as he wants it to be. Again, if he could see into the future, he would go ahead and get rid of everything which offends him. He would have no concern over whether a person could change or not. He would go ahead and zap the evil. But he can't see into the future, or know if and when a person might change his mind and decide to do things God's way. God has given everybody except his election freewill to do as they want. He sends prophets, preachers, witnesses, into the world to proclaim his message and places people in positions to make a choice. Some will choose God's way and some will not. If a person has all the knowledge of who and what God is all about and chooses Satan's way anyway, there's no more hope for him. These will be sent to the "Lake of Fire" after the Great White Throne Judgment! Meanwhile, their spirits will reside in a part of heaven reserved for such as chose this option as they wait for the Great White Throne Judgment. This is what the parable of Lazarus and the Rich Man was all about. It was given to show there are two parts to heaven.

Not a lot is given about what happens during the thousand-year reign of Christ in the Millennium. But this we do know; the elect of God can go to a loved one who didn't make the cut and try to persuade this loved one to accept Christ's way. I guess this is God's way of making right the hardships some of his elect have gone through. Anyway as it is given in Ezekiel, when reading of the things the elect can and cannot do, we read,

> And they shall touch no dead person to defile themselves: but for father, or for mother, or for son, or daughter, for brother, or for sister that hath had no husband, they may defile themselves. (Ezekiel 44:25)

When speaking of a "dead person", it is understood the scriptures are referring to the "spiritual dead" because in the Millennium everybody will be in a spiritual body and be alive until at least the "Great White Throne Judgment".

We are told all the land will be divided up among the peoples of the earth in whatever amount God deems each family will need. And the monetary system will be stabilized to where inflation and greed will not be tolerated. The amount of taxes or offering to the Prince is given and when this is to be given. The manner of worship is laid out. There will be no more denominations or different forms of worship or of things to be worshipped. God's feast will be reinstituted and kept throughout the years. We learn symbolically the earth will become similar to the "Garden of Eden" and healing and food will be plentiful. We are told the strangers living among the children of Israel will bare children still and will inherit their potion of the land. (Ezekiel 47:22)

The Chosen Nation Recalled and Blessed

God chose Abraham after the flood in Noah's time. He chose Abraham because he knew what spirit he had placed into the flesh body of Abraham. But, since Abraham was flesh and blood and had no recollection of what had transpired in the first earth age, God tested him before accepting this man to bring about the first part of his plan to redeem all of his wayward children back to him. God always tests the things he will use to bring about his will on earth. God tested Abraham pretty severely, even to the point of sacrificing his only son. (Hebrews 11:17) Abraham came through with flying colors; he obeyed God at ever command. And things or situations haven't changed; Christ said, "If you love me, keep my commandants". (John 14:15) We have to ingrain in our minds that Christ is the King and we are his subjects. Whatever he asks, we are to do without question. But a word of warning, make sure it is Christ who commands and not a fake claiming to be Christ.

Abraham produced Isaac and Isaac produced Esau and Jacob, who were twins. God rejected Esau and chose Jacob and Jacob produced twelve sons who became the head of the twelve tribes. God changed Jacob's name from Jacob to Israel as it is written in the book of Genesis:

> And God said unto him, thy name is Jacob: thy name shall not be called any more Jacob, but Israel shall be thy name: and he called his name Israel. (Genesis 35:10)

So God changed Jacob's name and used his twelve sons, who are Reuben, Simeon, Levi, Judah, Issachar, Zebulun, Joseph, Benjamin, Dan, Naphtali, Gad, and Asher to start up the tribe of Israel and their blood descendants make up the Nation of Israel. After the reign of King Solomon, the northern part of Israel separated itself from being ruled by Solomon's son and selected their own King under the leadership of Joseph's linage. The tribes of Judah and Benjamin stayed with Solomon's son and the capital city of Jerusalem. So now we have two Nations; one group of Israelites calling itself the Nation of Israel and the other group calling itself the Nation of Judah. The Nation of Judah later became known as the "Jews" after they returned from captivity in Babylon. Just keep in mind all Jews by bloodline are Israelites, but not all Israelites are Jews.

Along about now you're probably thinking we're going to get into this "Jew" thing; about how they are God's chosen people and all the trials and trouble they have in the world. Well. You're wrong! To began, the Jews are not God's chosen people; they are not even close. If you go by bloodlines, parts of the Jewish community are a small part of God's chosen people. The rest are outsiders and only claim Jewish heritage because they were born in the land of Judah. You see, there are more ways than one to become a Jew.

You can be born from a bloodline which runs all the way back to Jacob's son Judah. You can accept the Jewish faith by going through the rituals and rites, and you can also be a Jew by being born in the land of the Jews. Paul, considered himself a Jew, but he was also of the tribe of Benjamin as it reads in the book of Romans,

> I say, hath God cast away his people? God forbid! For I also am an Israelite, of the seed of Abraham, of the tribe of Benjamin. (Romans 11:1)

Did you catch what Paul claimed his heritage as being? Paul said he was an Israelite of the seed of Abraham; he was a Jew by religion only and even this was lost when he confessed his faith and loyalty to Jesus Christ. As Paul writes about Israel, keep in mind that at this time in history, the Israeli nation as such does not exist anymore. God has moved them by the Assyrians out of the "land of Israel" and scattered them through the Caucus Mountains into what is now called Europe and Russia. They have been mixed with so many different peoples until they have lost their national identity as God promised and wrote in the book of Zechariah, and it reads,

> Therefore it is come to pass, that as he cried, and they would not hear; so they cried, and I would not hear, said the Lord of Hosts: but I scattered them with a whirlwind among all nations whom they knew not. Thus the land was desolate after them that no man passed through nor returned: for they laid the pleasant land desolate. (Zechariah 7:13-14)

What did Christ tell the twelve he sent out preaching and healing? As it is written,

> These twelve Jesus sent forth, and commanded them saying, go not into the way of the Gentiles, and into any city of the Samaritans enter ye not: but go rather to the lost sheep of the house of Israel. (Matthew 10:5-6)

Who are God's chosen people? You should have picked up by now that they are Israelites. And where are the Israelites if they are not the ones residing in the new Nation of Israel? Well, I'm sure some of the ones residing in this modern nation of Israel are Israelites, but only the ones who can trace their bloodlines back to the founding Fathers of Israel; that is, Jacob's sons. Where are the rest of the Israelites located? One good clue is that we know they all descended from the Adam of the Garden of Eden. One of the translations from Hebrew to English of the name Adam is to show blood in the face; in other words, they are the peoples who blush when embarrassed. Of course, it is understood not all of the descendents of Adam are Israelites; only the ones who came through Jacob. As God said, they are scattered around the world but you will find most of them to be of European stock and they have settled in the America's and Australia, parts of Africa, Russia and everywhere. They don't know who they are; they have moved so much in the past centuries from place to place until their original National identity has been lost. The other Kingdom, the tribe of Judah has retained its identity and for the most part, they are the ones who have brought to life the modern nation of Israel.

But God will not leave this situation as it is. He has stated in his word he will put the whole house of Israel back together again in the last days or end times. He will recall his people, the Nation of Israel and bless them and forgive their sins. More about this promise is found in the book of Ezekiel where it reads with God speaking to Ezekiel,

> Moreover, thou son of man, take thee one stick, and write upon it, for Judah, and for the children of Israel his companions: Then take another stick, and write upon it, for Joseph, the stick of Ephraim, and for all the house of Israel his companions: And join them one to another into one stick: and they shall become one in thine hand. And when the children of thy people shall speak unto thee, saying, wilt thou not shew us what thou meanest by these? Say unto them, thus saith the Lord God; behold, I will take the stick of Joseph, which is in the hand of Ephraim, and the tribes of Israel his fellows, and will put them with him, even with the stick of Judah, and make them one stick, and they shall be one in mine hand. And the sticks whereon thou writest shall be in thine hand before their eyes. And say unto them, thus saith the Lord God; behold, I will take the children of Israel from among the heathen, whither they be gone, and will gather them on every side, and bring them into their own land. And I will make them one nation in the land upon the mountains of Israel; and one king shall be king to them all: and they shall be no more two nations, neither shall they be divided into two kingdoms anymore at all: neither shall they defile themselves anymore with their idols, nor with their detestable things, nor with any of their transgressions: but I will save them out of all their dwelling places, wherein they have sinned, and will cleanse them: so shall they be my people, and I will be their God. (Ezekiel 37:16-23)

So you see, God will recall his chosen nation at some time still in the future and will bring them to him and bless them and restore them to their land. When this will happen is not given in the bible; just that it will happen. A prophecy given in the book of Jeremiah was fulfilled in 1948 when the new nation of Israel was formed and this was a mile marker in the count down to the end of this physical age. The parable concerning the forming of the new nation of "Israel" speaks about two baskets of figs, one good and one bad, which are symbolic of the nation of Judah and the parable reads with Jeremiah speaking,

> The Lord shewed me, and , behold, two baskets of figs were set before the temple of the Lord, after that Nebuchadrezzar king of Babylon had carried away captive Jeconiah the son of Jehoiakim king of Judah, and the princes of Judah, with the

carpenters and smiths from Jerusalem, and had brought them to Babylon. (Jeremiah 24:1)

Jeconiah is the bloodline Christ descended from in the flesh. After he was deported to Babylon, Zedekiah was placed on the throne of Judah as a vessel pulpit king to Nebuchadrezzar king of Babylon. Zedekiah was the last official king of Judah; all his sons were slaughtered before his eyes and he was blinded and carried to Babylon to end his days there because he led a rebellion against the king of Babylon.

And now continuing with the parable of the two baskets of figs,

> One basket had very good figs, even like the figs that are first ripe: and the other basket had very naughty figs, which could not be eaten, they were so bad. (Jeremiah 24:2)

Jeconiah and the group of people with him carried away captive into Babylon are the good figs and the people left with Zedekiah are considered in this parable as the bad figs.

Continuing with the parable,

> Thus saith the Lord, the God of Israel; like these good figs, so will I acknowledge them that are carried away captive of Judah, whom I have sent out of this place into the land of the Chaldeans for their good. For I will set mine eyes upon them for good, and I will bring them again to this land: and I will build them, and not pull them down; and I will plant them, and not pluck them up. (Jeremiah 24:5-6)

Now a type of this happened seventy years later when Cyrus the Mede, released all of the tribe of Judah who desired to return to Jerusalem, the right to go and rebuild their city and Temple. But this was only a type; the real return will not take place until Christ returns as King of Kings. Only a few were given a heart to know the Lord at this time; just enough people to carry out God's plan in bringing himself to earth in the form of Jesus to fulfill his plan of redemption.

I'm sure some who read this material will disagree with me and that is ok with me if it's alright with God; he is the one who you need to satisfy. The reason for my earlier statement is by what the next verse reads,

> And I will give them a heart to know me, that I am the Lord: and they shall be my people, and I will be their God: for they shall return unto me with their whole heart. (Jeremiah 24:7)

This hasn't happened as yet and didn't happen when the Jews returned from Babylon. They weren't given a heart to know God then and not even now; some of this same bunch who returned from Babylon led the people into murdering the Lord Jesus. And what about the bad figs the parable speaks of? Continuing,

> And as the evil figs, which cannot be eaten, they are so evil; surely thus saith the Lord, so will I give Zedekiah the king of Judah, and his princes, and the residue of Jerusalem that remain in this land, and them that dwell in the land of Egypt: and I will deliver them to be removed into all the kingdoms of the earth for their hurt, to be a reproach and a proverb, a taunt and a curse, in all the places whither I shall drive them.. And I will send the sword, the famine, and the pestilence, among them, till they are consumed from off the land that I gave unto them and to their fathers. (Jeremiah 24:8-10)

Has this prophecy come true; check your history books? The peoples of Judah, now called Jews, have been removed into every land on the face of the earth. The Jews as a whole are regarded with a sneer and a caution to be on guard when dealing with them.

History show most countries didn't want them in their land or cities and held no concern whatsoever when they were mistreated or prosecuted. Hitler is credited with destroying over seven million of this people and we don't have actual numbers of the atrocities committed against this people in the intervening centuries since the Romans slaughtered the rebellious ones in the last uprising dated at AD 135. At that time, the Romans passed laws for it to be a crime for a Jew to enter Jerusalem and the surrounding countryside. The prophecy of the Jews returning to their own land was not fulfilled until 1948 when the modern Nation of Israel was established and God has said he will leave them there, much to the disgust of their surrounding neighbors who have tried unsuccessfully to eradicate them numerous times. Now then, is what I'm relating to you important? Christ tells all his follows to learn the parable of the fig tree. He didn't say maybe you should learn it; he said "learn the parable of the fig tree" (Mark 13:28)

Here are the words of Christ,

> Now learn a parable of the fig tree; when her branch is yet tender, and put forth leaves, ye know that summer is near: so ye in like manner, when ye shall see these things come to pass, know that it is nigh, even at the doors. (Mark 13:28-29)

A deeper learning about the fig tree would be to recognize God has chosen this plant for prophecy starting all the way back to the Garden of Eden when Adam and Eve used the fruit of the fig tree to make a poultice to cover their sin. (Genesis 3:7)

We have covered a lot of ground but the chosen Nation has not been recalled and blessed as yet. Only a part of the Nation has been recalled today and they are known as Jews for the most part. The rest of the Nation of Israel has yet to be recalled. I don't know God's timetable, but this recall may not be until after the Anti-Christ is defeated and the Millennium begins. We'll just have to wait and see. But as Christ said,

> Watch ye therefore: for ye know not when the master of the house comes, at even, or at midnight, or at the cockcrowing, or in the morning. (Mark 13:35)

Mankind Dealt with as a Whole:

We have been discussing the events of Israel being recalled and blessed; most of these times will not happen until after Christ has returned and locked Satan in the bottomless pit. Then Christ will recall his people from wherever they are scattered. This recalling will be in line with the overall theme of mankind being dealt with as a whole. Some of the people will be happy to see Christ on his throne and some will not be so happy.

We know from the book of Zechariah that the day Christ returns and his feet touch down on the Mount of Olives a great valley will be created running east and west through the mountain Jerusalem sits on. (Zechariah 14:4) This violent earthquake will announce the arrival of the King. At that moment also, all living people will be changed into a spiritual body (1 Cor. 15:51-52) and their flesh bodies will consume away as it is written in the book of Zechariah. (Zechariah 14:12) As Paul explains in 1 Corinthians, we have two bodies, a spiritual body and a flesh body. The spiritual body resides inside the flesh body and is only released when the flesh dies.

Let's read how Paul explains it in 1 Corinthians beginning in chapter 15 and verse 39 and continuing,

> All flesh is not the same flesh: but there is one kind of flesh of men, another flesh of beasts, another of fishes, and another of birds. There are also celestial bodies and bodies terrestrial: but the glory of the celestial is one, and the glory of the terrestrial is another. There is one glory of the sun, and another glory of the moon, and another glory of the stars: for one star differed from another star in glory. So also is the resurrection of the dead. It is sown in corruption; it is raised in incorruption: It is sown in dishonor; it is raised in glory: it is sown in weakness; it is raised in power: it is sown a natural body; it is raised a spiritual body. There is a natural body, and there is a spiritual body. (1 Cor. 15:39-44)

And skipping on down to verse 51, we pick up the thought line,

> Behold, I shew you a mystery; we shall not all sleep, but we shall all be changed, in a moment, in the twinkling of an eye, at the last trump; for the trumpet shall sound, and the dead shall be raised incorruptible, and we shall be changed. (1Cor. 15:51-52)

How many trumps are there? If you said seven, you are correct; so that makes the last trump the seventh, right? Remember, Satan's time on earth is the sixth trump and everybody knows six comes before seven and even a small child with tell you Satan comes before Christ.

As I said above, we have two bodies and after the change, we will have a spiritual body which will not wear out or get sick as long as we drink of the living water which flows from Mt Zion where Jerusalem sits. As it is written,

> And it shall be in that day, that living waters shall go out from Jerusalem; half of them toward the former sea and half of them toward the hinder sea; in summer

and in winter shall it be. And the Lord shall be King over all the earth: in that day shall there be one Lord, and his name one. (Zechariah 14:8-9)

This living water will keep spiritual bodies alive and healthy for the next thousand years as long as you come to Jerusalem once a year to pay homage to the King and to keep the feast of tabernacles. And,

> Whoso will not come up of all the families of the earth unto Jerusalem to worship the King, the Lord of hosts, even upon them shall be no rain. (Zechariah 14:17)

This rain is symbolic of the living water we discussed above.

OK, let's get all this in perspective; Christ has returned as King of Kings and tossed Satan's butt in the bottomless pit where he can't do anymore harm. The Holy Spirit has changed every living person in this flesh world into Spiritual people with a spiritual body. When Christ returned, he brought with him all the ones who were with him in paradise from the beginning of this earth age. The ones Christ brought with him have a spiritual body the same as all the peoples of the earth except, some of these have already been judged and justified by God. These will be used by Christ to keep order and also teach all the people who have not had a saving knowledge of Jesus Christ before. It doesn't matter when or where they lived. They could have lived ten thousand years ago or still have been living in the flesh when Christ touched down on earth. Male or female, or color of skin has no bearing; they could be blue, black, green, white, or purple, it makes no difference. Now, all will be taught the law and ways of God's kingdom and what God expects of each and every person.

The next thousand years, or the Millennium as some people refer to it, will be spent getting all the facts straight. There will no longer be any interference from Satan during this period of time. There won't be any "fallen angels" giving out the wrong message. These fallen angels have already been locked up and are waiting for their sentence of death to be carried out. They are "dead men walking" if you understand the phrase. For reference as to this being the way it will be is given in the book of Revelation several times. And they are listed here:

> And hath made us kings and priests unto God and his Father; to him be glory and dominion for ever and ever. (Rev. 1:6)

> And they sang a new song, saying, thou are worthy to take the book, and to open the seals thereof: for thou wast slain, and hast redeemed us to God by thy blood out of every kindred, and tongue, and people, and nation; and hast made us unto our God, kings and priests: and we shall reign on earth. (Rev. 5:9-10)

> Blessed and holy is he that hath part in the first resurrection: on such the second death hath no power, but they shall be priests of God and of Christ, and shall reign with him a thousand years. (Rev. 20:6)

Now, I ask you, what are the duties of a king and priest other then to keep order in the kingdom and discipline his people and the priest is there to teach God's word in the right way; chapter by chapter, verse by verse; so God's word will be in every mind.

Yes, I know there are a lot of unruly people in the world and after Christ returns with the bunch he has with him, there will be more. But, this is what the living waters are all about; if a person doesn't show up for teaching on schedule, the living waters will stop.

Remember, you have a spiritual body, not an immortal body. Spiritual means livable to die if God so chooses. As it reads in Matthew,

> And fear not them which kill the body, but are not able to kill the soul: but rather fear Him which is able to destroy both soul and body in hell. (Matt. 10:28)

During this thousand years time period, only a few choice ones will be allowed in the presence of Christ and they have a certain ritual to undertake in this service to Christ. As it is written in Ezekiel,

> But the priests the Levites, the sons of Zadok, that kept the charge of my sanctuary when the children of Israel went astray from me, they shall come near to me to minister unto me, and they shall stand before me to offer unto me the fat and the blood, saith the Lord God. (Ezekiel 44:15)

What's wrong with this picture? This world age is in the millennium and everything is in a spiritual body and there is no more physical fat or blood left on earth. The word "fat" is translated from the Hebrew word "cheleb" and literary means to be fat, but as used here should have been translated the "choicest part". And the word "blood" from above is translated from the Hebrew word "dam" and means blood, but it's the kind of blood which causes death. In other words, pure substance as the juice of the grape and is used here symbolic of Christ's blood which he shed.

Continuing in Ezekiel,

> They shall enter into my sanctuary, and they shall come near to my table, to minister unto me, and they shall keep my charge. And it shall come to pass, that when they enter in at the gates of the inner court, they shall be clothed with linen

garments; and no wool shall come upon them, whiles they minister in the gates of the inner court and within. They shall have linen bonnets upon their heads, and shall have linen breeches upon their loins; they shall not gird themselves with anything that causes sweat. And when they go forth into the outer court, even into the utter court to the people, they shall put off their garments wherein they ministered, and lay them in the holy chambers, and they shall put on other garments; and they shall not sanctify the people with their garments. (Ezekiel 44:16-18)

This is a little hard to grasp, but we'll give it a try. The reason the priests have to

change clothes is because if an unjustified or sinner in a spiritual body comes in contact

with Christ or even have clothes which may have brushed against Christ, this "touching"

will give eternal life to the person who comes into contact with such apparel. This is the

same reason Adam and Eve were driven out from the Garden of Eden. They had sinned

and if they came in contact with the tree of life, they would have become immortal but

still have the desire to sin and rebel. What would God do with such people? As it is

written in Genesis,

And the Lord God said, behold, the man is become as one of us, to know good and evil: and now, lest he put forth his hand, and take also of the tree of life, and eat, and live forever: therefore the Lord God sent him forth from the garden of Eden, to till the ground from whence he was taken. (Genesis 3:21-23)

As we continue:

And they shall teach my people the difference between the holy and the profane, and cause them to discern between the unclean and the clean. And in controversy they shall stand in judgment; and they shall judge it according to my judgments: and they shall keep my laws and my statutes in all mine assemblies; and they shall hallow my Sabbaths. (Ezekiel 44:23-24)

So now you know the duties of the kings and priest who serve under Christ. The kings will be in charge of the divisions of the land so every family has their rightful share. The manner of worship and the offerings will be spelled out so everybody knows what they are expected to do.

After the Kingdom is established, Christ will locate all of his children which are scattered all over the earth. He will captivate their hearts and bring them into his loving arms as it is written,

> For, behold, in those days, and in that time, when I shall bring again the captivity of Judah and Jerusalem, I will also gather all nations, and will bring them down into the valley of Jehoshaphat, (God has judged) and will plead with them there for my people and for my heritage Israel, whom they have scattered among the nations, and parted my land. (Joel 3:1-2)

And as it is written in Matthew,

> When the son of man shall come in his glory, and all the holy angels with him, then shall he sit upon the throne of his glory: and before him shall he gather all nations: and he shall separate them one from another, as a shepherd divides his sheep from the goats: and he shall set the sheep on his right hand, but the goats on the left. Then shall the King say unto them on his right hand, come, ye blessed of my Father, inherit the kingdom prepared for you from the foundation of the world; (Matt. 25:31-34)

So you see, Christ will have a large job on his hands; straightening his kingdom out and making it to God's approval for all eternity.

Part Five

Satan Bound and the Consequences:

So far, we have touched lightly on the role of Satan. In the next few pages, we'll look at this character in more depth. I have often wondered why a beautiful child could turn so bad until finally God had no choice but to condemn his child to death. (Ezekiel 28:18)

Satan is first mentioned in the first book of the bible in the Garden of Eden as the serpent who seduced Eve and Adam into disobeying God and therefore becoming sinners. We have all read the story and artist have tried to depict the sin in progress by symbolizing the sin as a forbidden fruit of a tree. In actuality, their sin was totally different; that is, their sin was of a carnal nature in that Satan had a sexual relationship with both Adam and Eve. The fig tree is used throughout the bible in prophecy because of the first use of its fruit. After the sin was committed by Adam and Eve, they tried to hide what they had done from God by making a poultice of the figs themselves and using this mixture to cover their private parts. The private parts are the parts of their bodies which had been used to commit the sin. I know the English translation doesn't tell this type of story but if you take the time to go into the Hebrew and translate from the Hebrew dictionary the exact words, this is the story you have laid before you. I recommend the original Strong's concordance before today's scholars started editing it.

Alright; even though Satan is first mentioned in Genesis, his story doesn't start there. I think it would be correct to say his beginning is first mentioned in the book of Job. God is talking to Job about the beginning of everything; a time several billions of years ago. God asks Job where he was when God made everything including the earth if he was so smart. God ask Job,

> Whereupon are the foundations thereof fastened? Or who laid the corner stone; when the morning stars sang together, and all the sons of God shouted for joy? (Job 38:4-7)

Notice, the scripture said "all the sons of God" meaning Satan was among them since he also is a son of God. Keep in mind Satan and all the angels were created before the earth and the heaven described in the first verse of Genesis. Reasoning for referring to this understanding is because we are now going to the last book of the bible and see a little more about the "fallen" son of God.

We see in this chapter the beginning of God's plan for his wayward children to be reconciled back to a favorable place in God's kingdom. Let's look at the scripture and then we'll talk about it. The verse reads,

> And there appeared a great wonder in heaven; a woman clothed with the sun, and the moon under her feet, and upon her head a crown of twelve stars: and she being with child cried, travailing in birth, and pained to be delivered. (Rev. 12:1-2)

We know this is all symbolic because no person could be clothed with the sun or have the moon as its footstool.

Ok, here we go: you can agree or chose not to agree. The woman is symbolic of our heavenly Father having all knowledge. This is represented by the woman being clothed with the sun; the sun being wisdom or knowledge. The moon is always a representative of earthly things and physical needs or wants just as the sun represents a higher plane of thinking and wisdom. The moon is symbolic of the physical earth with Satan as the prince of this world, and throughout the bible, Satan's times or events are always given in moons.

The bible informs us the stars are always Gods angels or messengers. Since we have a crown of twelve stars, we can conclude they portray a jury box or witnesses to Gods plans about to be instituted symbolized by the woman or event being in pain to be enacted. What is the jury sitting in witness for? Remember the moon under God's feet; Satan has been brought up on charges of rebellion and judgment is to be rendered. But Satan is not the only one on trial here; it is all the children who followed in his rebellion. God is revealing his plan to redeem his children to the angels who helped stop this attempted overthrow of God's government.

What is this plan God has in his mind; nothing short of the birth of this physical age to bring all his wayward children through so they can decide who they want to have as their King; God or Satan? I hope you make the right choice.

The next verse gives us another reaction; not everybody is happy about the impending event about to take place. We read,

> And there appeared another wonder in heaven; and behold a great red dragon, having seven heads and ten horns, and seven crowns upon his heads. (Rev. 12:3)

In the ninth verse of this same chapter we are told the different names given to Satan and we see "great dragon" is one of them. Since Satan is described as the "great red dragon", we can be assured he is not happy with what's taking place. The seven heads could only be referring to districts he controls along with the ten horns being his cohorts in power and the different offices they hold by the use of the etymology "seven crowns" on their heads.

The next verse gives us some insight into the charges against Satan and his followers. We read,

> And his tail drew the third part of the stars of heaven, and did cast them to the earth: and the dragon stood before the woman which was ready to be delivered, for to devour her child as soon as it was born. (Rev. 12: 4)

We know Satan doesn't have a tail even though some artists draw him with one and also the horns. This is all symbolic of his character and so we'll know who the bible is relating too. The tail drawing a third of the stars is letting us know Satan convinced and deceived a third of God's children into following him and rebelling against God their Father. And now at this time in history, Satan knows what is at stake. He is totally against what is about to happen and he will stop at nothing to keep the events from taking place. The phrase, "did cast them to earth" means Satan's followers left God's kingdom and came to earth to live and serve with Satan.

The last part of this verse is relating to the Nation of Israel as being the woman in this case of bringing forth. The Nation of Israel brought forth the Christ child and although Satan was unable to stop the birth of Christ, he tried hard through Herod to have this baby killed as soon as it was born.

Next, we are assured the scripture refers to Christ by the statement,

> And she brought forth a man child, who was to rule all nations with a rod of iron: and her child was caught up unto God, and to his throne. (Rev. 12:5)

His first attempt at stopping God's plan was in the Garden of Eden. Satan knew that if he could deceive this new creation of God into disobeying the Lord's directive, they would become sinners. (Romans 6:23) And therefore Adam would not be suitable for God's to use in reclaiming his children, who had become outcasts. God's purpose was to bring his sinning children into this earth age inside a flesh body. Their flesh minds would not retain any knowledge of the acts carried out before this age started. Then they could be reconciled back to the Father sinless at the death of the physical body. If this plan had

worked, the sentence of death would be carried out on Satan and his bunch, since they

were the guilty party in leading so many of God's children astray.

But the plan failed because of Satan's intervention and now God would have to have a
savior, or a substitute to pay the debt of sin against all his children. Because as it reads,
> And almost all things are by the law purged with blood; and without shedding
> of blood is no remission. (Hebrew 9:22)

God himself chose to be that sacrifice by coming into this flesh age in the body of

Jesus and allowing himself to be put to death on the cross.

Satan didn't stop with Adam and Eve. He instigated numerous angel cohorts into

coming to earth and seducing the daughters of Adam and producing children from this

union. This hybrid flesh on earth was an abomination to our heavenly Father and thus,

our Father used the flood of Noah's days to destroy the hybrids from the face of the earth.

Our bible reference is the six chapter of Genesis, and it reads,

> And it came to pass, when men began to multiply on the face of the earth, and
> daughters were born to them, that the sons of God saw the daughters of men that
> they were fair; and they took them wives of all which they chose. And the Lord
> said, my spirit shall not always strive with man, for that he also is flesh: yet his
> days shall be an hundred and twenty years. There were giants in the earth in those
> days; and also after that, when the sons of God came in unto the daughters of
> men, and they bare children to them, the same became mighty men which were of
> old, men of renown. (Genesis 6:1-4)

Satan believed he could contaminate all the female offspring of Adam with the

"fallen angels" and therefore none of the physical women in this line of Adam would be acceptable for God to bring himself into this flesh world. But, Satan didn't get the job done and when there was only one pure blooded family left on earth, God brought the flood on the earth and destroyed all the work of Satan.

The next time we look in on Satan's doings is in the book of Job. There he and God have a contest if you can accept it, about whether Satan can convince Job to renounce God. Satan believes he can put Job into such a state physically and mentally until job will curse God. After the first couple of chapters in the book of Job, we have the next thirty-six or so chapters where Satan is using Job's so called friends to convince Job he is a sinner. They state half-truths, lies, and a little of everything without success. Finally, Satan enters the conversation as the fourth friend to try his own hand at convincing Job that he is a sinner. No luck on this one; Satan just doesn't get it, does he? God's children love God and would never curse God. They might have sin in their lives, but they still love God and have respect for him. (Job 3:37)

We see this wily deceiver in the wilderness trying his hand at deceiving Christ; that is, God in the flesh. What happens? Satan tries to get Christ to worship him and to break one of God's laws by quoting scripture to Jesus, the person who wrote the scripture. Of course, Satan didn't quote the verses of the bible correctly, but changed a word here and there or left out a part of the overall verses. Jesus wasn't fooled for a second. But instead of arguing with Satan about the bible, Christ quoted scripture to refute the sayings of

Satan. A lesson to be learned here is to never argue with the Devil, you'll lose unless Christ is speaking through you. (Matt. 4:1-11)

After losing to Christ, we hear no more of him openly in the scriptures, but we see his handy work behind the scenes as his children plot and finally succeed in getting Christ murdered through the death of the cross. As the old saying goes, Satan shot himself in the foot this time. He not only provided the sacrifice God wanted to atone for his wayward children, but also got himself a death penalty in the boot by being a party to murder. Now God can carry out the death sentence placed on Satan anytime he wants to. But not yet, there are still a few things God has for Satan to do. God is still using the Devil to test his children to see how many of them can be influenced to do things Satan's way.

Even though we don't hear of Satan's presence anymore in the bible, he is spoken of in the future sense in the book of Revelation and in the book of Ezekiel. These we will cover and we'll check out the satanic prophecies given in the bible concerning what he'll be doing in our lives during the two centuries since Jesus walked this earth in the flesh.

John, the servant of Christ, gives his account of a vision he received from Christ and wrote it in a book we call Revelation. This vision is given so God's children will have an understanding of the events to take place on earth before Christ returns from the Father. A chronological order of things to happen before Christ sets up his kingdom on this earth.

We're not going to have a study on the whole book of Revelation now, but just certain parts which deal with Satan directly, and how he plans to take over this earth as his own. After Christ has given John a message for the seven churches of Asia, he starts to open a scroll one seal at a time. I might mention here this scroll and seals are more then likely the same scroll and seals shown to us in the biblical book of Daniel. At the end of this book, Daniel was told not to worry about the prophecies at this time because these prophecies were for some future date. As The Angel told Daniel,

> Go thy way, Daniel: for the words are closed up and sealed till the time of the end. (Daniel 12:9)

Why were the words sealed up unto the time of the end from Daniel? My opinion, and my opinion only, it's because there was a chance, a small chance the people living on earth at the time Jesus walked its surface in the flesh could have accepted him as the Messiah. And if they had, all the events hidden in the sealed scroll of Daniel's vision wouldn't have come to pass.

As I stated earlier, God gives his children "freewill" and he doesn't know what they will do until they do it. If everybody didn't have freewill, there would be no reason to have this flesh age in the first place; God would just zap the undesirables and the rest would be with God eternally. I'm sure he knows most of the ones who will not change and who will not love him. But there is always a chance these will come to their senses and change their outlook on life. This is one of the reasons it is written the angels rejoice over one sinner who learns to trust their Father.

The first seal shows a white horse with the rider caring a bow and wearing a crown. He looks official and he is wearing white which symbolizes purity, and according to Zechariah 6:3; this "white horse" is one of the four spirits of Heaven and is used by God to bring peace in the place where it is sent. Perhaps, this white horse given in Revelation is symbolizing the building of the early church founded by Peter in Jerusalem. We know the early church grew rapidly for quite a few years until the Roman emperor Nero blamed the burning of Rome on Christians.

When Christ opened the second seal, an image of a red horse appeared with a great sword and power was given him to take peace from the earth. And so it was, from the second century Ad until about six hundred AD, fighting in the church was a normal thing and fighting in the Empire was continually being waged. The sword as stated in Revelation 1:16 represent doctrine being taught. In Isaiah 49:2, a prophecy about Christ states, "he has made my mouth like a sharp sword". The sword is his mouth or you could say a mighty speaker spreading doctrine. The doctrine could be right or it could be false.

The black horse of the next seal represents famine and hard times symbolized by the rider having a pair of balances in his hand. In past history, balances were used to measure portions of substances to figure the price to be paid. For those of you who have never heard of, or used balances, they are a type of measuring scale. An object of known weight was placed on a pan hooked up to a seesaw device. The substance to be weighted was placed into another pan on the other end of the seesaw and more was added until the pans were identically level with each other. Occasionally, part of the substances was removed to make the pans balance with each other; hence the name balances.

And then we come to the fourth seal and this rider is riding a horse which has not been mentioned in the bible before. This rider sits on a pale horse, but his name was "Death"; so, we know without a doubt the rider is none other then Satan himself. We are told in Chapter 2 of Hebrews that Death is one of the names of Satan. The symbolism should be obvious; the picture reeks of dying and if you fall for the deception Satan spreads, you are dying. Look at what happens, twenty-five percent of the earth believes his lies and the lying doctrine he spreads is represented by the sword. Don't forget, the sword is a person's mouth speaking with a persuasive voice. (Rev. 6:7-8) Hitler was a type; you do remember the way his public speaking swayed the crowds and the masses of people he deceived, followed him right into the graves. Don't be led astray by false teachings; study your bible and know what God's word says and what God expects from you.

Even though we looked at four different horsemen, these are just symbolic of the different offices Satan controls. He's still the prince of this age and he'll reign until Christ comes and removes him from office. When you think this way, the idea of God's people being strangers in this world makes sense. The fact we are looking for a new home is understandable. As Paul writes in Hebrews,

> These all died in faith, not having received the promises, but having seen them afar off, and were persuaded of them, and embraced them, and confessed that they were strangers and pilgrims on the earth. (Hebrews 11:13-14

We are now approaching the present time and what do we see happening with Satan? Reading further into chapter 12, we find there is a war raging in Heaven and this war has been going on for some time. Let's read how the bible gives it,

> And there was war in heaven: Michael and his angels fought against the dragon; and the dragon fought and his angels, and prevailed not; neither was their place found any more in heaven. And the great dragon was cast out, that old serpent, called the Devil, and Satan, which deceived the whole world: he was cast out onto the earth, and his angels were cast out with him. (Rev. 12:7-9)

Just how long has this war been waged? I don't know, but we read of it being fought in the book of Daniel and that was almost 3000 years ago.

> Then said he unto me, fear not, Daniel: for from the first day that thou didst set thine heart to understand and to chasten thyself before thy God, thy words were heard, and I am come for thy words. But the prince of the kingdom of Persia, (Iran) withstood me one and twenty days: but lo, Michael, one of the chief princes, came to help me; and I remained there with the kings of Persia. (Daniel 10:12-14)

This is the angel Gabriel speaking and he has come to tell Daniel and the rest of us what is to take place on earth in the final days of this flesh life. The next few verses are Daniel's reply to how unworthy he is, but we'll pick up Gabriel's speech starting with verse 20 and it tells us,

> Then said he, know thou wherefore I come unto thee? And now will I return to fight with the prince of Persia: and when I am gone forth, lo, the prince of Grecia shall come. (Daniel 10:20)

So you see a war and fighting has been going on in Heaven for a long time; maybe from the overthrow of Satan's first earth age kingdom. I don't know and it's not recorded when this war started.

After Satan and his angels are booted out of Heaven onto the earth, they will begin their campaign against God's Elect. These elect are the same ones who stood against Satan in the first earth age in helping overthrow this deceptive villain. God's elect are at a disadvantage because they don't remember the first earth age or the events which occurred in it. But they know and have an understanding of God's word and how to tell the fake from the real. But, Satan knows who these people are because he still remembers them from his fall in the first earth age. And, he will come after them to try and change their minds about him.

The book of Daniel lets us know he will come in peacefully and prosperously; (Daniel 11:21) so, he won't seem to be a villain and why should he? He's coming as a good guy and claiming to be Jesus Christ returning for his church. His lies will include spreading doctrine to which all religions are part of his church. When he sits on his throne in Jerusalem, he will have set aside for him by God, a seven year span to see how many of the peoples of the earth he can fool. He'll spend the first three and half years setting up his total control of the world. He will rule the military and all countries through the ten fallen angels he brings with him. And make a guess at who his biggest ally will be in this take over? We have a description of her given in seventeen chapter of Revelation. It reads,

> And there came one of the seven angels which had the seven vials, and talked with me, saying unto me, come hither; I will show unto thee the judgment of the great whore that sits upon many waters; with whom the kings of the earth (financial, political, education, religion) have committed fornication, and the inhabitants of the earth have been made drunk with the wine of her fornication. So he carried me away in the spirit into the wilderness: And I saw a woman sit upon a scarlet colored beast, full of names of blasphemy, having seven heads and ten horns. And the woman was arrayed in purple and scarlet color, and decked with gold and precious stones and pearls, having a golden cup in her hand full of abominations and filthiness of her fornication: And upon her forehead was a name written, MYSTERY, BABYLON THE GREAT, THE MOTHER OF HARLOTS AND ABOMINATIONS OF THE EARTH. And I saw the woman drunken with the blood of the saints, and with the blood of the martyrs of Jesus: and when I saw her, I wondered with great admiration. (Revelation 17:1-6)

We have seen this beast before. This beast was first shown to us in Revelation 13:1-7. Now we get a better picture of the beast as it tries to hide in the wilderness. The beast is in the wilderness because it claims to be "Christian" and the wilderness is where God has hid his elect. (Rev. 12:4) We are told the woman is that great city which reigns over the kings of the earth. In John's day, this city could only be Rome because Rome ruled everything, but in truth, the woman symbolically stands for confusion. Originally, the great city was Babylon which in itself as translated into English means "confusion". In modern times, the city is still Rome but more precisely, Vatican City, which sits inside Rome. We are told in the bible, the water represents peoples and multitudes and nations and languages. The Catholic doctrine, which has its roots in the ancient Babylon Mystery

Religion of Nimrod, controls a huge population worldwide. Their influences over the "kings of the earth" are an indisputable fact. This religious system will support Satan and his supernatural cohorts in taking control of the world. John knows he is looking at a vision, but he still cannot believe God will allow this fake system to last until the end of this age.

God declares anything or any person who changes the worship of himself to something idol or a person as being harlots. We are not talking about physical people, but ideas and religious beliefs. Look around you, what groups of people have caused the worship of Christ to be in vain or to be secondary to their goals. These are all harlots in God's eyes, but which of the religions of the earth deceives more people then the rest. This one is the "mother" of harlots. She claims to be "Christian", but the formation of this "church" is the same as the ancient "mystery" religion Nimrod of the Old Testament used to control the peoples of his day. We know Babylon translated from the Hebrew is "confusion" and confusion is Satan's main tool to be used on all peoples.

Originally, Satan was to have seven years to rule on earth and get as many people to follow and worship him as he could, but because he is so slick in his deceptive devices, Christ shorten his time to only five months of full power. Christ did this for the elect's sake. Satan is so convincing, Christ felt too many of his election would be drawn into Satan's camp and would commit the unpardonable sin. This bunch, God's elect, are the only ones who can commit the unpardonable sin because they have already been judged

and justified and now if they follow Satan, it will be unforgivable for them.

The time of Satan's total dictatorship being shortened is given in Matthew, and we

read,

> And except those days should be shortened, there should no flesh be saved: but
> for the elect's sake those days shall be shortened. (Matt. 24:22)

Basically the same scripture is given in Mark, chapter 13. We will find the length

Christ shortens the time period of Satan's full control in the book of Revelation. And we

read,

> And to them it was given that they should not kill them, but that they should be
> tormented five months: and their torment was as the torment of a scorpion, when
> he strikes a man. (Rev. 9:5)

And again for emphasis,

> And they had tails like unto scorpions, and there were stings in their tails: and
> their power was to hurt men "five months". And they had a king over them, which
> is the angel of the bottomless pit, whose name in the Hebrew tongue is Abaddon,
> but in the Greek tongue hath his name Apollyon. (Rev. 9:10-11)

Both of these names when translated into English are destruction or the destructor,

which is Satan's main occupation. That is, he's here to destroy God's plans.

Satan's reign as the dictator of earth will not be a bad government as men look at the

way they think governments should be. Satan will be pleasing to everyone, and he will have total control of all the armed forces of the world. Any little hot spot will immediately be put down and not by heavy force. But the perpetrators will be brought before Satan and his cohorts for a new indoctrination or "brain washing"; whatever you call it, a flower by any other name is still a flower. In other words, they will be brought into the system and deliberately serve this system. Of course God's election are the exception, they know the truth and won't budge to Satan's coercing. If they do, it's eternal death for them.

So you'll be prepared, let me give you an example of how it's going down. I know it's given in the bible, but a lot of people don't realize what they are reading. Let's begin our reading in the book of Matthew and Christ is doing the speaking,

> And ye shall be brought before governors and kings for my sake, for a testimony against them and the gentiles, (He's talking about the future government of Satan and his cronies, the ten kings he brings with him, and you being put on trial for your convictions of the real Christ.) But when they deliver you up, take no thought how or what ye shall speak; for it shall be given you in that same hour what ye shall speak. (Don't try to have a prepared speech; trust your heavenly Father and just answer the questions put to you the best you can. The Holy Spirit will be the one doing the talking, so all you'll need to do is be strong and have enough nerve to open you mouth and talk. If you freeze up and don't speak, the Holy Spirit can't use you to put Satan where he belongs.) For it is not ye that speak, but the Spirit of your Father which speaks in you. (Matt. 10:18-20; emphasis mine)

Perhaps, you are saying to yourself, "I'm not going before the Devil". It doesn't matter what you thing, Satan already knows who you are. He remembers you from the first earth age when you fought against him there. Keep in mind, he is supernatural and knows all that happened when he was defeated the first time and who caused it. He's not stupid and he won't come after you with armed force. Your own family will turn you over to the authorities. As it is written,

> And the brother shall deliver up the brother to death, and the father the child: and the children shall rise up against their parents, and cause them to be put to death. (Matt. 10:21)

Now a normal family will protect its members from any danger, but where they perceive there is no danger and spiritual discernment is the issue, things can be quite the contrary. And for the record, who or what is death; it is just one of Satan's names. Some of the family will think Satan is Christ and will want you to be saved and have the rewards of Heaven. This is the reason Christ said,

> For I am come to set a man at variance against his father, and the daughter against her mother, and the daughter-in-law against her mother-in-law. And a man's foe shall be they of his own household. (Matt. 10:35-36)

It doesn't really matter, it is God's plan for some of his elect to be tested and tried to show Satan he can't win. If you are one of these, go gladly and be happy God believed in you enough to choose you for his work. Eventually, Satan will get tired of hearing from God's elect and his inability to convert them to his way of thinking and the bible says he will kill two witnesses in a world wide arena with the world watching. I guess he'll have the television crews set up all over the earth to record and televise anything he wants the world to see. We are not told who or what the two witnesses are, but let's read from His word first and then discuss this subject some more. We read,

> And I will give power unto my two witnesses, and they shall prophesy a thousand
> two hundred and sixty days, clothed in sackcloth. These are the two olive trees,
> and the two candlesticks standing before the God of the earth. (Rev. 11:3)

Candlesticks, we are told in the first chapter are God's churches; so we can be assured one of the two witnesses will come from the church and I'm sure it will be one of the churches or both churches which pleased Christ, because of what they taught. Or maybe, it will be the message these churches teach; in other words, the bible. I don't know for sure, but it's a possibility. And the other witness; in Jeremiah, God calls the nation of Israel a green olive tree and in the Psalm 52:8, David claims to "be like a green olive tree" to God. Could one of the witnesses be from the tribe of Judah or the Nation of Judah and the Nation of Israel? Or maybe, the witnesses are what each of these countries represents. And while we are guessing; and that's all I'm doing, could the two witnesses be Moses and Elijah, both being the leaders of the law and prophets of God. These two appeared with Christ on the Mount of Transfiguration. Could these two be sent back to witness against Satan? Elijah never died in the flesh, but was taken up in a whirlwind. And we are not sure about Moses, God wouldn't let anyone besides him bury Moses. The possibility of Moses not dying is given in the book of Jude where it reads,

> Yet Michael the archangel, when contending with the devil he disputed about the
> body of Moses, dared not bring against him a railing accusation, but said, the
> Lord rebuke thee. (Jude 1:9)

It seems from this dialog that Satan wanted to see the body of Moses and couldn't find it. The reason for this search is because he wanted to know if Moses, a sinner, had been admitted to Heaven and Abraham's boson when he didn't warrant it. In other words, was God unfair? Michael wouldn't discuss the subject, but told Satan to talk it over with God. We need to do the same when we are having discourses with Satan.

We can conceivably use any number of scenarios to say who the two witnesses are, but until they arrive, we could all be wrong. What we need to do is watch and wait and be ready when they come because it will mark the final days of this earth age. And the bible tells us,

> And when they have finished their testimony, the beast that ascended out of the bottomless pit shall make war against them, and kill them. And their dead bodies shall lie in the street of the great city, which spiritually is called Sodom and Egypt, where also our Lord was crucified. (So we know this is taking place in Jerusalem.) And they of the people and kindred's and tongues and nations shall see their dead bodies three days and a half, and shall not suffer their dead bodies to be put in graves. And they that dwell upon the earth shall rejoice over them, and make merry, and shall give gifts one to another; because these two prophets tormented them that dwelt on the earth. And after three days and a half the Spirit of life from God entered into them, and they stood upon their feet; and great fear fell upon them which saw them. And they heard a great voice from heaven saying to them, come up hither, and they ascended up to heaven in a cloud; and their enemies beheld them. And the same hour was there a great earthquake, and the tenth part of the city fell, and in the earthquake were slain of men seven thousand: and the remnant were affrighted, and gave glory to the God of heaven. (Rev. 11:7-13)

Some theologians believe this seven thousand to be most of the "fallen angels" who arrived on earth along with Satan when he was kicked out of Heaven. They are probably right because all the angels who refused God's plan of reconciliation have been sentenced to death and that sentence would more than likely be carried out the minute Christ returns to the Mount of Olives. The actual number "seven" could be symbolic in that seven means spiritual completeness. Whatever; I teach these seven thousand are all the fallen angels who came with Satan to earth when he was ejected from Heaven.

Just because Christ has arrived doesn't mean the Devil is going to just up and lay down and surrender; no, he's going to fight. The bible tells us he gathers all his forces to fight against the coming savior and as it reads,

> And I saw three unclean spirits like frogs come out of the mouth of the dragon, and out of the mouth of the beast, and out of the mouth false prophet, for they are spirits of devils, working miracles, which go forth into the 'kings of the earth' and of the whole world, to gather them to the battle of that great day of God Almighty. And he gathered them to gather into a place called in the Hebrew tongue Armageddon. (Rev. 16:16)

These unclean spirits are symbolic. And the things they came out of are symbolic. What the vision instructs us in is the propaganda being broadcast unto the world's people. We know the dragon is Satan and the beast is the military which Satan controls and the false prophet is just what it says. It is false doctrine being spread around the world that Satan is the Christ. We know what the kings of the earth portray, that is, religion, finance, government, and education. This vision John sees and writes about is to prepare us for the fact that the whole world joins Satan and his government. That is, the entire world except God's elect who know what's going down at this time. Are you one of the ones who will stand against Satan or will you be one of his warriors and fight the true Christ? Only you can make that choice.

Continuing in the bible,

> And I saw the beast, (One world government system) and the kings of the earth, and their armies, gather together to make war against him that sat on the horse, (White horse, Rev. 19:11-16) and against his army. And the beast was taken, and with him the false prophet that wrought miracles before him, with which he deceived them that had received the mark of the beast, (this beast is Satan) and them that worshipped his image. These both were cast alive into a lake of fire burning with brimstone. (Rev. 19:19-20)

Keep in mind the false prophet and the first beast was only offices; the false prophet represents the religious beliefs on earth at this time and the other beast is the government controlling the earth at this time. Both of these are done away by the symbolic "casting into the lake of fire". Who and what is the lake of fire? I will remind you of Hebrews 12:29, where it reads, "For our God is a consuming fire". If you didn't quite catch it; God is the "lake of fire"; he is the "hell" most preachers mistakenly preach about.

And what happens to Satan; since he lost the war, did he make his get away? No! But, let's read again in the bible. It reads,

> And I saw an angel come down from heaven, having the key of the bottomless pit and a great chain in his hand. And he laid hold on the dragon, that old serpent, which is the Devil, and Satan, and bound him a thousand years, and cast him into the bottomless pit, and shut him up, and set a seal upon him, that he should deceive the nations no more, till the thousand years should be fulfilled: and after that he must be loosed a little season. (Rev. 20:1-3)

OK, we know from this scripture, Satan won't be ruling "Hell" or any thing else for at least a thousand years. This time period is called the "Millennium" and God has set it aside for teaching and learning discipline. We have covered a lot of this earlier in this study. One thing we didn't cover is the lock-up of Satan. He'll be in the pit alright, but

he'll be visible to any and all who wish to take a good look at him. As it reads in Isaiah,

> Hell (this word Hell is translated from the Hebrew word Sheol and it only means a holding place; like for instance, the wrong side of the gulf in Heaven from the part where Christ lives.) from beneath is moved for thee to meet thee at thy coming: it stirs up the dead for thee, even all the chief ones of the earth; it hath raised up from their thrones all the kings of the nations. All they shall speak and say unto thee, art thou also become weak as we? Art thou become like unto us? Thy pomp is brought down to the grave, and the noise of thy viols: the worm is spread under thee, and the worms cover thee. (This is all symbolic; it's to let us know Satan has no power anymore and he is as a dead person.) How art thou fallen from heaven, O Lucifer, son of the morning! How art thou cut down to the ground, which did weaken the nations! For thou has said in thine heart, I will ascend into heaven, I will exalt my throne above the stars (angels) of God: I will sit also upon the mount of the congregation, in the sides of the north: I will ascend above the heights of the clouds; I will be like the most High. Yet thou shall be brought down to hell, to the sides of the pit. They that see thee shall narrowly look upon thee, and consider thee, saying, is this, the man that made the earth to tremble, that did shake kingdoms; that made the world as a wilderness, and destroyed the cities thereof; that opened not the house of his prisoners? (Isaiah 14:9-17; emphases mine)

After Satan is locked up into a pit like the animal he is, people from all over the earth

will come by and stare at him in wonder; they will find it hard to believe this little man

put the world through such woe.

The Earth Restored and Blessed: The Millennium

The war between Christ and Satan has wreaked havoc on everything; rotting flesh is

everywhere. Why? The spirit has left the flesh body and has been turned into a spiritual

body. The flesh has been left to rot where it was discarded. We will have a large clean up

job on our hands. And as Zechariah tells it,

> And this shall be the plague wherewith the Lord will smite all the people that
> have fought against Jerusalem; their flesh shall consume away while they stand
> upon their feet, and their eyes shall consume away in their holes, and their tongue
> shall consume away in their mouth. (Zechariah 14:12)

And again in Isaiah,

> Their slain also shall be cast out, and their stink shall come up out of their
> carcasses, and the mountains shall be melted with their blood. (Isaiah 34:3)

And again in Ezekiel,

> And it shall come to pass in that day, (day of the Lord) that I will give unto Gog a
> place there of graves in Israel, the valley of the passengers on the east of the sea:
> and it shall stop the noses of the passengers: and there shall they bury Gog, and all

his multitude: and they shall call it the Valley of Hamongog. And seven months shall the house of Israel be burying of them, that they may cleanse the land. (Ezekiel 39:11-12)

Christ will establish his seat of authority or throne in Jerusalem on Mt Zion and from there direct all the activities of the world. His messengers will carry his orders to all parts of the earth while a specified group will have burial duty. There will be a great stink in the land because of all the dead people and animals lying everywhere rotting away and this mess will have to be cleaned up. The ones who will be teachers will be setting up areas for teaching and the troops of Christ will be rounding up and seeing everybody has a place of learning to attend.

The earth itself will be renewed; the deserts will bring forth grass. All the land shall be turned as a plain from Geba to Rimmon south of Jerusalem and it shall be inhabited. (Zechariah 14:10) We are not told a whole lot about what will be happening during the Millennium except for the teaching of who and what God is and the way he expects his government to reign. Some people will take to it like ducks to water and others will not be happy in their situation. The good side is there will be plenty for all to have, including food, water, and most anything your heart could ask for. The down side is that some people just can't or won't adjust to authority. These will more then likely be unhappy and the Millennium will seem as a prison to them.

Satan's Final Rebellion:

At the end of this thousand year period, Satan will be released from his prison of the

bottomless pit. God will allow him to roam the earth again and to persuade as many as he

can to accept him and his way of doing things. Strange as it might seem, millions will

like what they hear and decide to join the ranks of Satan again. I'm sure most of these

will be Kenites, (Cain's descendants) but there will be a lot of others too. You've heard

the old story, "some people just can't stand success". Anyway, this is how the bible puts

it,

> And when the thousand years are expired, Satan shall be loosed out of his prison, and shall go out to deceive the nations which are in the four quarters of the earth, Gog and Magog, to gather them together to battle: the number of whom is as the sand of the sea. And they went up on the breath of the earth, and compassed the camp of the saints about, and the beloved city: and fire came down from God out of heaven, and devoured them. And the devil that deceived them was cast into the lake of Fire and brimstone, where the beast and false prophet are, and shall be tormented day and night for ever and ever. (Rev. 20:7-10)

Or, if you want a better detail of Satan's end and the reasons why God completely

destroyed this son of his, we can read of this end in the book of Ezekiel, and it says,

> Son of man, take up a lamentation upon the King of Tyrus, and say unto him, thus saith the Lord God; thou sealest up the sum, full of wisdom, and perfect in beauty. (Ezekiel 28:12)

Here Satan is called Tyrus; which when translated from the Hebrew means 'rock'.

Our 'Rock' is Christ, but Satan tries to copy Christ in all his deceptions as we read in

Deuteronomy, Chapter 32. We read,

> He is the Rock, his work is perfect: for all his ways are judgment: a God of truth
> and without iniquity, just and right is he". (Deut. 32:4) And again, "Of the rock
> that begat thee thou are unmindful, and has forgotten God that formed thee. (Deut.
> 32:18)

And again,

> How should one chase a thousand, and two put ten thousand to flight, except their
> rock had sold them, and the Lord had shut them up? For their rock is not as our
> Rock, even our enemies themselves being judges. (Deut. 32:30-31)

I just wanted to show you there are two rocks in the bible; One Rock is Christ and

the other rock is Satan, trying to imitate our Lord.

And now continuing in Ezekiel,

> Thou has been in Eden the garden of God; every precious stone was thy covering,
> the sardius, topaz, and the diamond, the beryl, the onyx, and the jasper, the
> sapphire, the emerald, and the carbuncle, and gold: the workmanship of thy
> tabrets and of thy pipes was prepared in thee in the day that thou was created.
> (Ezekiel 28:13)

All these stones and jewelry are given in symbolic sense to show nothing was spared

in making Satan the most perfect individual in God's creation. He was created to rule

earth and if he had done the job right, he would be on the throne forever. But he didn't do

his job the way God laid it out for him. So now, God had to come into this flesh world physically as Jesus, and qualify to replace him by leading a sinless life and satisfying the needs of the people. All rulers are supposed to take care of their people and not the other way around. Continuing:

> Thou art the anointed cherub that covers; and I have set thee so; thou was upon the holy mountain of God; thou has walked up and down in the midst of the stones of fire. Thou was perfect in thy ways from the day that thou was created, till iniquity was found in thee. (Ezekiel 28:14-15)

Satan was right beside the throne of God. He was one of the guards placed there to protect the seat of the Almighty. He was stationed there also to receive any instruction God wanted carried out in his kingdom. You see, God controls the entire universe and Satan's job was to take care of earth and this solar system which was part of his domain. But, instead of taking care of business, he decided he could run it better then God and his pride convinced him to rebel against his creator. Because he was so slick, he conned a third of his subjects to follow him in this rebellion. God couldn't put up with this rebellion and by the same token, he didn't want to destroy a third of his children who were deceived by Satan. Thus, the need for the flesh age of the earth, so each person would have an opportunity to decide for themselves who they would trust and follow, God or Satan. Continuing:

> By the multitude of thy merchandise they have filled the midst of thee with violence, and thou has sinned: therefore I will cast thee as profane out of the mountain of God: and I will destroy thee, O covering cherub, from the midst of the stones of fire. Thine heart was lifted up because of thy beauty, thou has corrupted thy wisdom by reason of thy brightness: I will cast thee to the ground, I will lay thee before kings, that they may behold thee. (Ezekiel 28:16-17)

Satan's first step away from God was pride. He became full of himself and he began to think more of himself then of the responsibilities God gave him. His main task was taking care of God's children and their needs. We all know the saying, "power corrupts and total power corrupts totally", and so Satan became totally corrupted. He was the most beautiful of the angels and had the wisdom of God to use, but his wisdom was used to take everything for his own use. Another old proverb comes to mind, "you ride highest just before a great fall" and Satan's fall from "king of earth" to imprisonment in the "pit" for all to gander at will be a great fall.

The next verse reads,

> Thou has defiled thy sanctuaries by the multitude of thine iniquities, by the iniquity of thy traffick; therefore will I bring forth a fire from the midst of thee, it shall devour thee, and I will bring thee to ashes upon the earth in the sight of all them that behold thee. (Ezekiel 28:18)

This supernatural person in his supernatural body will be destroyed by the fire of the Holy Spirit and this event will take place in the sight of all the onlookers in the area. Once this takes happens, the deceptive power of Satan will be gone forever and so will the persona of his office. Satan won't be ruling anything else ever again because he will have been blotted out. Even the memory of him will cease in our minds as God renews all things. And finally,

> All they that know thee among the people shall be astonished at thee: thou shall be a terror, and never shall thou be any more, (Ezekiel 28:19)

Never again will we have to put up with somebody like Satan throughout all eternality. The sad part of this end is the loss of all of God's children who chose to follow Satan and the way of the world. This bunch, consisting of millions will be lost also in the "Lake of Fire" because they followed Satan and chose his way of life instead of God's way. Sad, isn't it? Which bunch will you be in when Satan is released to try the nations for the final time? The choice is yours and has always been your choice. Didn't you know you choose where you want to go, Heaven or Hell?

Part Six

The New Heaven and the New Earth: The Day of the Lord.

Rev.21, 22, 2 Peter 3:12-13; Isa. 65:17, 66:22.

When Satan is gone and Christ is seated on his throne, our Father will start to renew the earth as it was in the first earth age. The water in the oceans will return back to the atmosphere from where it was before the moisture descended to the earth to bring about the flood in Noah's days. All the deserts will bloom with flowers, trees and grass again. The whole earth will be as the "Garden of Eden" once more. All the cavernous animals will become gentle and grass eaters.

As it is stated in God's word,

> The wolf also shall dwell with the lamb, and the leopard shall lie down with the kid; and the calf and the young lion and the fatling together; and a little child shall lead them. And the cow and the bear shall feed; their young one shall lie down together: and the lion shall eat straw like the ox. And the sucking child shall play on the hole of the asp, and the weaned child shall put his hand on the cockatrice' (snake) den. They shall not hurt nor destroy in all my holy mountain: for the earth

shall be full of the knowledge of the Lord, as the waters cover the sea. (Isaiah 11:6-9)

And again for emphases:

The wolf and the lamb shall feed together, and the lion shall eat straw like the bullock: and dust shall be the serpent's meat. They shall not hurt nor destroy in all my holy mountain, saith the Lord. (Isaiah 65:25)

And in that day will I make a covenant for them with the beasts of the field, and with the fowls of heaven, and with the creeping things of the ground: and I will break the bow and the sword and the battle out of the earth, and will make them to lie down safely. (Hosea 2:18)

We'll have the same old earth to live on, but it will be renewed. After God gets through with the job of renewing this planet, the earth will be a brand new place to live.

As it reads in His word,

For, behold, I create new heavens and a new earth: and the former shall not be remembered, nor come into mind. (Isaiah 65:17)

And again,

For as the new heavens and the new earth, which I shall make, shall remain before me, saith the Lord, so shall your seed and your name remain. (Isaiah 66:22)

And also in the New Testament,

Nevertheless we, according to his promise, look for new heavens and a new earth, wherein dwells righteousness. (2 Peter 3:13)

And in the book of Revelation,

> And I saw a new heaven and a new earth: for the first heaven and the first earth were passed away; and there was no more sea. (Rev. 20:1)

In reading these last few verses which are scattered in different places in the bible, some of you may think God is going to do away with this earth and create a new one. But that's not the way it's going down. What is going to happen is that God plans to put everything back where it was when he first created this universe. The water in the oceans and rivers will vaporize and return back to the atmosphere to the place from which it came. The earth will water itself as in the days before Noah's period of the flood. Everything will return to its original luster and beautiful design. We will have vehicles similar to the ones described in the first chapter of Ezekiel and will be traveling throughout the universe.

In the meantime, the Holy Spirit or comforter will keep everything on an even keel. The Spirit will see to it that God's plan for his children and this age run on schedule and according to his purpose. At the end of this age, everything which offends will be total erased and we will not even remember that the undesirables every existed.

Pretty fascinating, isn't it; to read and understand what this whole flesh age is all about. This book will hopefully give you all the information you will need to understand the purpose God had in putting all his wayward children through this earth age. You have always had a choice as to whom you wish to serve and love, Satan or God. It is understood some will only wish to serve themselves, and this is your choice. But Satan chose that direction and the bible informs you of the facts concerning his demise in the "Lake of Fire" or as a lot of preachers still preach, in "Hell". Will you surrender your life to a loving Father who will see to it your hearts desires are met, or will you continue in your rebellious ways and die? The choice is yours.

THE SONG OF MOSES

In the 15th chapter of the book of Revelations, beginning with the 2nd verse; we read, "And I saw as it were a sea of glass mingled with fire: and them that had gotten the victory over the beast, and over his image, and over his mark, and over the number of his name, stand on the sea of glass, having the harps of God. And they sang the song of Moses the servant of God, and the song of the Lamb, saying, great and marvelous are thy works, Lord God Almighty; just and true are thy ways, thou King of saints. (Rev. 15:2 and 3) From earlier chapters of Revelation, we can understand the beast listed here is none other then Satan who had tried to take Christ's throne on earth. The scripture lets us know these people standing on the sea of glass have fought against Satan and his un-holy Angels and are winners. The scripture also tells us they sang the "Song of Moses" and the "Song of the Lamb". We have the praise song to the Lamb as the verse continues; but, what about the "Song of Moses". It is not given here. Why? This song has been given way back in the book of Deuteronomy. You should be familiar with it as one of God's Elect; but in case you missed it in your bible study, you can find it beginning with the last verse of chapter 31 and continuing to verse 44. We are going to take this song of Moses and study it verse by verse so there will be no misunderstanding in your mind about who and what God is telling us through Moses. We read,

And Moses spake in the ears of all the congregation of Israel the words of this song, until they were ended. (Deut. 31:30)

Give ear, O ye heavens, and I will speak; and hear, O earth, the words of my mouth. My doctrine shall drop as the rain; my speech shall distil as the dew, as the small rain upon the tender herb, and as the showers upon the grass: (Deut. 32:1&2)

God wants the heavens and earth to be witness to the words God will speak through Moses. What happens when it rains? The ground soaks up all it can hold and then the water spreads ever where as it drenches all things it touches. So is God's doctrine, but the words are not hard to hear. They are gentle and light as the morning dew and invigorate the soul as a summer shower does on herbs and pastures.

Because I will publish the name of the Lord: ascribe ye greatness unto our God. (Deut. 32:3)

To "publish" the name of the Lord is to introduce our Deity to the people. But it means more than that, in that it means to call upon, to proclaim, to witness. In my words, the Lord is present and watching all that transpires. It is really God speaking and honor is to be given him as a famous guest speaker. After all, God doesn't need us; we need him.

He is the rock, his work is perfect: for all his ways is judgment: a God of truth and without iniquity, just and right is he. (Deut. 32:4)

God has set forth a plan to reconcile all his wayward children back to himself. He has outlined this plan in the word of God of which we know as the Bible. Part of this overall plan is given in this "Song of Moses"; it will go well for you if you will take the time to read this plan and familiarize yourself with it contents and its symbols. This song is the "Key of David" mentioned in several places throughout the bible.

They have corrupted themselves; their spot is not the spot of his children: They are a perverse and crooked generation. (Deut. 32:5)

What generation are these peoples? Better yet; what peoples have continually fought against God's way of life? Who looks to material substances for their security and pride of life? Perhaps you are thinking that today this description fits a vast majority of peoples on this earth. Yes, you are right. They are a very smart people in the ways of the World and have been cunning enough to survive throughout history. I could give you their family name, but you wouldn't recognize it in modern society. So, let's look in the word of God at some of their ancestors.

The first person in the flesh body to go against God was Cain. This son of Satan murdered his twin brother Abel. He wasn't repentant or ashamed and God expelled him from the "Garden of Eden" and left him to his own devises. The scriptures tell us he went into the "land of Nod" and took a wife. His wife was of the people God created on the six day of rejuvenation of this planet as described in Genesis 1:26-27. We are told in the bible that Cain and his descendants were very skilled in the ways of the flesh world more so then Adam's children from Seth as shown in Genesis 4:17-23.

Christ's servant,

David B Hathcock

February 6, 2012

About the Author:

Mr. Hathcock was born in 1938 near the end of the "Great Depression" just outside of Ripley, Tennessee. Times were hard and money was almost nonexistent. His people were traditional farmers and a formal education beyond the "reading, writing, and arithmetic" was not needed by most at this time in history. He finished Ripley High School with grades good enough for him to be admitted into the University of Tennessee where his major was in Civil Engineering.

He was able to only attend school for a couple of years before the money ran out. He had received an inheritance from an "adopted" uncle, but this small gift only carried him for a couple of years in college. While in school, the first "dawning's" of a literary gift were evident as he made his way through the first two years of college English.

After he left school and for the next fifty or so years, he made his way through life and the world mostly learning about life in a school of hard knocks. He worked all over the U.S. and traveled as far north as Alaska and into southward as far as Mexico. The world is a great teacher if you listen to it's lessons and don't repeat your mistakes.

He served in the US Army at Ft. Carson, Colorado for three years which was during the Vietnam era. He was stationed there during the Cuban missile crisis and the assassination of President John F Kennedy. In 1964, he was discharged honorably with a rank of Specialists 5, E-5.

Later, at the age of 32, he married Katherine A. Harrison from Ripley and they were blessed with two children, a boy and a girl. The boy was named David A. Hathcock and the girl was named Jessica N. Hathcock. There are two grand-daughters from the union of Jessica and her husband, Mac Raymond. The grand-daughters are named Emmalee Madison and Kaylee Beth Raymond. All of David's family live and work around Anderson County, SC.

In the year 2000, he retired and went into Real Estate sales with his wife Kathy and started writing on when time permitted. This is the third book to be published; the other two books currently on the market at "A Path Thru the Weeds" and the "Way of Cain".

These books and other material can be viewed at his web site, www.DavidHathBooks.com/ or he can be contacted through email address, DavidHath@msn.com.

Mr. Hathcock is currently working on new material to be released sometime in the near future.